To my Lee Lee

── STAY ──
HUNGRY

Just because i love your belly
so much and your apetite even
more :-) I though your main
eating champ (other-than me)
could give you some tips :) haha

Enjoy your read my darling :D

Dan Dan xxxx
and
FURIOUS PETE

LIONCREST
PUBLISHING

CONTENTS

INTRODUCTION

I can't say I ever aspired to be a competitive eater. Taking down massive quantities of food really, *really* fast wasn't something I dreamed of as a kid. In the same way, I never expected that health and fitness would become my life's true passion. And if you had told me that I would build my career on a combination of those things, I probably would've thought you were a crazy person.

As far as childhood and family life goes, mine was about as normal as it gets. I was always kind of shy growing up (though thankfully that got better as the years went on), and I was never really that outgoing or adventurous. If a "sporty nerd" is a thing, then that's what I was. I was on the fast track to studying engineering, wanted to work for NASA, and loved math and science, but I also loved playing sports. I had a great group of friends, but we never did anything too wild. I definitely wasn't the craziest guy in the books, and I wasn't a party animal. I was more of a homebody and loved being around my family. I was the only child, and my parents and I were really close. Our life was normal and comfortable.

Then everything went wrong.

I was sitting in my high school chemistry class when the door to the classroom opened and an aide handed my teacher a note. Almost everyone in the class had stopped what they were working on because a mid-class note from the front office meant that—for better or worse—someone was going to get to skip the rest of class. My teacher's brow furrowed as he read what was written on the paper. Then he glanced in my direction.

"Peter, can you come up here for a second?"

I set down my pen and approached his desk. He leaned closer and, with his voice much quieter, said, "You need to go down to the office. Your father is there, waiting for you."

My dad? Why was he here in the middle of the afternoon? I turned on my heel and started walking toward the door of the classroom.

"Peter," my teacher called after me. I stopped and turned around. "You'll need to take your things with you."

I had no idea what to expect as I walked toward the office at the front of the school. Why would Dad have come to the school in the middle of the day? My mind raced with possibilities, most of them unpleasant.

My father had recently been hospitalized after a manic episode. We were told he had been diagnosed with bipolar disorder and that, though he could manage his swings with medication and some therapy, there would always be a chance that another episode could happen again. Was it possible that it had happened already? Where was my mom?

My father was standing by the door when I got there. He seemed totally fine. Though as I got closer to him, I realized he looked terrified.

"Pete, there you are. You're all set with the office," he said as I reached for the door. "I already signed you out. We gotta go." He was walking quickly toward the parking lot, already a few steps ahead of me.

"What's going on?" I asked as I hurried to catch up with him.

"It's Mom, Pete. She had to go to the hospital."

My mother had been diagnosed with multiple sclerosis a few years prior, and in the weeks since my father's diagnosis, she had been having a couple issues with her moods. She had already gone to see her doctor, who also found some problems in her pancreas and gallbladder but cleared her to go back home. Then she had been fine until the last day or so, when she started getting headaches.

I hadn't given the headaches much thought, not even that morning when Mom was still in bed when I left for school. Growing up, my mother would have headaches pretty often, even migraines, so it wasn't out of the norm to see her laid out for a day or two from time to time.

This time was different. Now my mom was in the hospital, connected to machines and moving in and out of consciousness. She looked small, vulnerable. It shook me up to see her this way. I couldn't escape the feeling that I had always been able to successfully fight off before: *I could lose my mom.*

I had always been closest to my mother. She and I shared a similar outlook on life, a similar sense of humor, and she always just seemed to understand me. She could sense my mood or whether something was bothering me, even if I didn't know what it was, and she somehow always knew whether I wanted to talk about it or be left alone. I couldn't fathom what my life might look like without her. But now as I sat next to her hospital bed, I couldn't help but think about it.

After a few days, Mom got the go-ahead to leave the hospital. She had to take it easy, but the weeks that followed were uneventful.

Then, I found myself sitting in the doctor's office. His gloved hands were pushing firm circles on my throat, just under my jawline. I winced and pulled back as a dull pain rippled through my head. I had been fighting a cold since my mom's hospital stay and now it had turned into the flu. I was normally a quick healer, but I just couldn't seem to bounce back from this one. Then one morning my lymph nodes had swollen up so much you could see them sticking out of my head, both lumps clearly defined and looking angry.

"That's it. I'm making you an appointment with the doctor," my mom said.

"Okay," I said as I painfully swallowed a sip of orange juice. I never liked going to the doctor, but I was so ready to be done with this cold that I didn't even fight her on it. Now what we both thought was going to be a routine appointment seemed to be turning into something bigger.

The doctor started talking about blood work, samples, lab tests, and a biopsy. "Wait, wait," my mom interjected, "what is all this for?"

"Well, we won't know until we run some tests," he said as he handed some forms over to us, "but we want to make sure that the cells in your lymph nodes aren't cancerous. Your symptoms are all in line with Non-Hodgkin's Lymphoma, which is very serious and..." He kept talking, but I didn't hear a word he said. The room seemed to come to a complete standstill. *Lymphoma? Cancer? But this is just a cold!*

"So, what is our next step?" my mom asked him. "What do we have to do?"

The doctor gave us the name of several specialists that I would have to meet with so they could take tissue samples and blood samples and perform a series of tests to figure out whether I had cancer and, if so, how serious it was so they could then determine my treatment options. He spoke about the diagnosis as if it were a foregone conclusion and the only task at hand was to determine what kind of cancer I had. It could be days, weeks, or even months until I had my answer and could know what was next for my life. Was it Lymphoma? Was it another kind of cancer that had already spread to my lymph nodes? Would I have to go through chemo? Would I have to drop out of school while I was being treated? Could I die?

"You'll know as soon as we do," the doctor said, handing me a stack of referrals.

My mom and I walked out of the office and got into the car. As we each closed our doors, shutting out the noise outside, a thick silence settled over us like a blanket. Mom fumbled with her keys before inserting them into the ignition, turned the car on, but then didn't shift it into drive. She sat with her hands at ten and two, staring at the dash. Then she glanced my way. "Pete..."

I shifted in my seat, turning my body toward the window. The last thing I wanted to do was talk about what the doctor had to say, or whether I should skip school for the week, or how we should tell my Dad. I didn't want to talk at all. Mom sensed it right away.

"...I'm thinking I'll run and grab us some sandwiches. I'll just put yours in the fridge until you're hungry." And with that she reversed out of our parking space.

I was completely numb. I had no idea whether I was supposed to be thinking or feeling a certain way, but I was pretty sure I wasn't doing it right. In movies and TV, a cancer diagnosis was usually met with tears, bolstering an internal strength or reaching out for comfort from the nearest loved one, and then making a vow to fight; there was always some kind of emotion at least—but I couldn't muster up anything at all.

As we drove, I moved completely into my own head, thinking about the little pieces of experience with cancer I had before. There wasn't much and none of it was good. The only thing I really knew about it was that people died from it more often than not. My Uncle John had died of lung cancer when I was little and my grandmother, my mom's mom, had died of stomach cancer before I was born.

Two years earlier, one of the girls in my class, Kelsey, lost her mom to breast cancer. Her mom's cancer had been caught early in Stage 2, and she was expected to come out of it okay. I remembered seeing Kelsey's mom at the grocery store and thinking that she didn't look sick. She just looked kind of tired, and her hair was very short.

Then something changed really fast. Kelsey started missing a lot of class, and we were told that her mom was in the hospital. My mom learned that she had gone into the hospital to have her lymph nodes removed, but her doctors discovered that the cancer had already spread to them. From there, her cancer had moved to different places in her body. When I asked whether Kelsey's mom would be okay, my mom simply replied, "What she has is very aggressive." Just a week or two later, my mom told me that she had died in the hospital. Kelsey didn't come back to class until the next year.

That was just a few months after she was diagnosed, and her doctors told her that she would be able to fight it, I thought as we made our way home. She probably went to the doctor and was told that she needed to run through some extra tests, just like I had been. Her tests confirmed the doctor's suspicions, just like we were now waiting for mine to do, then she got sicker and sicker until she died. *That's what cancer does.* I could feel a little sting behind my eyes at the thought and immediately shut my brain back down. I stared out the window and went back to not thinking anything at all.

Once we got to the house, I immediately walked up to my room. My mom reminded me about the sandwich in the fridge but said little else. She could sense that I didn't want to talk about it (or anything else), and I doubt she would have known what to say in that moment if I had. I lay down in my bed and stared up at the ceiling. I knew Mom was calling my dad to give him the news, and I didn't know what would be worse: having to talk about it when he got home, or sitting around the table in tense silence. I realized I didn't really care either way.

CHAPTER 1

CAMP

A couple of weeks later, I got an answer from all the lab work that had been submitted: inconclusive. I was going to have to start over.

In that time, my lymph nodes had gone back to normal. My flu-like symptoms had subsided. I was perfectly capable of going back to school, playing sports, and basically picking up like nothing had happened. It was terrifying to think that in spite of all outward appearances of good health my body could still be fighting a cancer we couldn't find.

My parents were livid. "How could he have just thrown out 'cancer' if he didn't know for sure yet?" My father's face almost turned purple as he talked about it. "He had nothing to go on but swollen lymph nodes, and he tells our son it's Lymphoma. That doc should have talked to us instead of scaring him." My mom nodded as he spoke. I don't think I had ever seen them so angry. I, on the other hand, still wasn't feeling much of anything.

I was in a deep funk. I had been in it since the week of my first doctor appointment, and now learning that I was going to have to keep waiting—and that I was going to have to do all those tests again—certainly didn't help. I wasn't angry with my doctor the way my parents were, nor was I sad about being kept in limbo. It was as though my mind took stock of everything that had happened in the past few months—my father being hospitalized and diagnosed with bipolar disorder, my mother being hospitalized after a series of issues related to her MS, and then being told that I had cancer—and decided to shut down for a while.

There were moments here and there when the switch in my brain flipped, and, for a minute or so, I could feel my fear hit me like a train. I felt completely uprooted, like there wasn't anything I was able to control in my life or in my family's life. These things had happened (or were happening) to me and my family, and there wasn't anything that I could do about it. There wasn't anything I could do to make my mom healthier; there was nothing I could do to help my father.

The possibility that I had cancer showed me that I ultimately didn't have any control over what happened to me either. I was young, healthy, and played sports everyday, and *still* my tests could come back saying "cancerous" as easy as they could say "benign". There wasn't a damn thing I could do either way. My brain seemed to cycle the same thought again and again: *what's the point?* My parents, my mom especially, didn't really know how to read my lack of emotion.

"Honey," she said one night over dinner, patting my hand. Then she hesitated, as though she were thinking about what to say next. "Do you still want to go to camp? You don't have to if you don't want to."

Months before any of this happened, I had signed up to be a camp counselor at Camp Ekon, an awesome sports camp out on the lake in Muskoka. I was going to be gone all summer, away from my parents for three months. It was something I had been really looking forward to, but now I wasn't sure if I even wanted to anymore. I also wasn't sure that I could back out this close to the camp's start.

"Might be nice," my dad added, seeming to be taking a cue from my mom. "You can get a change of scenery. Keep busy and have some fun for the summer."

I thought it over for a second and then nodded my head. "I'm still going to go," I said, feeling more like I was watching myself talk than actually saying the words. "I would feel bad if I backed out."

"Okay," my mom said with a smile. "I think it will be a good thing to get out of here and take a break for a while."

And I suppose it was. Camp was basically non-stop activity from the day I arrived. First, we had to go through counselor training, learning the ins and outs of our roles within the camp and all the different games, sports, and activities we would be teaching the kids. We learned the structure, the different rules (for us and the campers), and worked our butts off getting the camp ready for Drop-off Day. Once the kids all arrived, then we were extra-busy with our responsibilities to all of them, entertaining them and making sure they didn't do any of the idiotic things kids seem to be magnetically attracted to. The distraction was nice; it felt good to put my mind on other things, but I wasn't my same old self.

By the time we reached the middle of the summer, the other counselors had started to catch on to my weird moods. They realized something was going on with me, but no one could put a finger on what it was. Whatever was bothering me, they probably figured, was too serious for me to want to talk about over s'mores. So one day, the director of the camp took the more formal approach and sat down with me to check in.

"Pete, is everything okay?" she asked. "You don't really seem to be engaged with these campers. It seems like you're preoccupied, like your mind is elsewhere while we're all working."

I wasn't surprised by the sit-down. I suppose part of me was even expecting it to happen sooner rather than later. The truth was I hadn't had much energy lately, and it was getting harder and harder to go full throttle on the enthusiasm. "Yeah, of course, everything's fine," I told her. "I've just been thinking a lot about my parents."

I told her that they had been going through some health issues and that I was worried about them. I didn't mention my own cancer scare or the fact that I hadn't felt right since. She nodded as she listened and told me that I could come to her if I ever wanted to talk about it further. My answer had satisfied her and explained away most of the issues that had come to her attention. It probably didn't address why I was so often absent during mealtimes, but she never asked about it specifically. I was glad she hadn't.

Despite the rigorous scheduling the camp laid out for us counselors, I still felt like my life was out of control. Little by little, however, I found that there were a few options that I did feel like I could control. Especially when it came to my food. It started small, by putting back a portion of what I had put on my plate and refusing all sweets—a simple exercise in control. It felt good, calming, to exert my will on something and see the outcome play out as expected. I couldn't control what happened in my life, but I could control what went on my plate. And so I started exercising this control (and tapping into that good feeling) by restricting my food more and more each day. Now, in the last four weeks of camp, I was no longer sitting with the campers passing around burgers and pasta and everything else that was coming to the table. I had a new routine.

I started going to the back of the kitchen, and I would cut myself some salad with dressing then walk back out to rejoin the group. Then one day I was holding the dressing bottle in my hand and decided to restrict that too. I looked up at the large, red-capped plastic containers of spices lining the aluminum shelf above the prep table I was standing at, my eyes scanning from right to left: *clove, cinnamon, cayenne.* Cayenne pepper would work. I grabbed the container and started dusting the otherwise bare lettuce leaves. I took a bite, nodded, and walked back out to rejoin the group. From that point forward, I skipped the dressing entirely, instead covering the leaves with black and cayenne pepper and a squeeze of lemon or a piece of tomato if I could find one. I knew it was weird—it didn't even taste good, just spicy. But it had become a habit at this point, a comfort, and even though I had almost no energy, I wasn't about to change it.

I came home from camp in late August, with my final year of high school starting in early September. I brought my routine of restricting and changing up my food home with me too. It still gave me that sense of control, even though I had little else to distract me while I waited for the doctor to call.

The call finally came at the end of September: there was no cancer. I was perfectly healthy. The doctor had been wrong the entire time.

My mom and I both sat in the doctor's office in disbelief as he delivered the results: "Great news! My initial thoughts were incorrect. Your tests have all come back just fine." All I could think as he spoke was, "*This is it? After months of thinking I was sick, of the tests and blood work and biopsies, now everything is fine?*" I felt relieved, of course, but I didn't feel happy. Once again, I walked out of the doctor's office feeling numb. When I got home, I went for a long run and skipped dinner.

The sense of control I had so desperately craved over the last few months didn't come back with the good news that my health scare was in fact just a scare. The combination of my fears for my parents and for myself, coupled with the feeling that I had no control in my life had pushed me past my tipping point, and, unfortunately, my mind had taken over with this need to restrict. From there, things just started getting worse and worse. I couldn't ease my brain or the thoughts that flooded through it. I couldn't ignore the impulse to control my eating. The fact that I didn't have cancer didn't matter anymore.

CHAPTER 2

OBSESSION

When school started, a new set of stresses came along with it: a new schedule, a course load of college prep classes, and of course trying to get into university. Under the weight of exams, applications, and essays, I felt like I was losing the small grip I had found while I was at camp. Day by day, I started restricting my food more and more. I was putting cayenne pepper on everything, since most of what I ate was bland and tasteless. I also started exercising a lot, all intense cardio and long runs. At first, I was running five miles, then I would run ten miles every day, all while eating virtually no food.

Lunch at school was a Diet Coke. I wouldn't pack or buy myself anything else. If my mom packed me something, I would give it away or throw it out. It started to become a game for me, an extra challenge in life to just restrict what went into my body. The more I was restricting, the more I felt I was succeeding. And if I failed to restrict on a certain day, exceeding a certain amount of calories, then I felt like I was a failure.

The weird thing was, I knew that what I was doing wasn't good for me. I just didn't really care. Instead, I put my focus on the challenge aspect of restriction, which was becoming more and more challenging as my appearance changed more and more. The last thing I wanted was to have to answer questions about what I was doing or why I was doing it, and I absolutely didn't want my friends to know what I was doing. So, I took a lot of steps to hide it all the time.

"Pete, we're grabbing pizza. You in?" My buddy Rik asked me as we were leaving school for the day.

This was the kind of invite that always made me feel anxious. Of course I wanted to go hang out with my friends, but I wasn't about to let greasy food throw off my calorie count for the day. I had a couple options available to me, the easiest of which was to just swing by my house then tell the guys I already ate when I met back up with them. "Yeah, sure thing. I just gotta swing by my house first."

"Nah, come on man," Rik said. "Everyone's going right now."

There wasn't much I could say to that. So much for my escape plan. We went out to the pizza place, grabbed a table big enough to hold our whole group. My mind was working furiously the entire time, trying to think of a way to not eat the pizza. While everyone else was ordering, I noticed the grocery store on the other end of the parking lot. *Bingo.*

I jumped out to the grocery store and bought a head of iceberg lettuce. When I walked back into the pizza place and sat down, Rik asked, "Where'd you go? We all ordered already."

"That's all right," I replied. "I'm good." As their slices all arrived at the table, I pulled out my lettuce and started munching on the leaves while they were eating. Obviously this drew some questions. "What the hell, Pete? What are you doing?" Half the table was looking in my direction.

"Oh, I like the crunch," I replied.

"But that's not even real food," Rik said. "Isn't lettuce, like, almost entirely water?"

"Yep," I answered, "I was thirsty." I would always make up reasons why I was eating what I was eating and why I was enjoying it. It was half the battle in keeping other people from digging too deep into what I was doing.

The other half was keeping myself warm. At school, I would get super-cold all the time. My body temp was really low because I wasn't giving it enough calories, so I would pile on layer after layer of shirts. And as an added bonus, because I was wearing so much, it didn't look like I was that skinny or that I was losing weight. You could tell by my face that something wasn't right, of course. I was gaunt and really pale, but my overall body composition didn't seem like it was getting smaller because of all the layers I was adding on top of it.

Still, I could never get warm. Being freezing and hungry all the time had become the norm for me, so much so that I didn't even notice anymore if my behavior looked weird. But my friends were now noticing.

When I sat down next to Rik at lunch one afternoon, he shot me an annoyed look. I opened my Diet Coke and took a sip. "What?"

"Is something wrong, dude? Are you sick or something?" Rik asked.

"No. Why?" I took another sip and tried to look like I had no idea what he was talking about. It wasn't hard. I genuinely had no clue why he was asking.

"When you came over to my place yesterday, you were white as a ghost. I was drinking a pop and eating some popcorn and asked you if you wanted some. All you wanted was a boiling hot cup of water. I thought you were joking, but when I handed it over, you chugged it like it was a beer or some juice. I was like 'what the hell?' but then instead of explaining why you were acting like a weirdo. You went over to the couch and covered yourself with five blankets. You were asleep, like, two minutes later."

I knew I had fallen asleep at Rik's and missed most of the movie we were supposed to watch. I remembered being freezing, but the rest was drawing a blank. "Sorry, man. I wasn't trying to be weird. I just—yeah—I think I'm fighting something." I turned and coughed into my shoulder for effect.

While my body was gradually diminishing, there was another

force in my life that was getting stronger and stronger: the voice in my head. It controlled me, telling me, *"You're fat. Everyone is judging you. You're disgusting."* I had never been overweight but, by virtue of my height, had always been bigger than the other kids in my class. Now this voice was telling me that was a problem, and I believed it.

Little by little, that voice in my head became the dominating force in my life. I was no longer in control of my body, the voice was. And it was destroying me, inside and out.

Fat. Useless. You're never going to amount to anything. You'll be a loser for the rest of your life. Every action I took was wrong; the voice would tell me to do the opposite of what I wanted. Nothing I did was ever enough; the voice would tell me to do the more extreme thing. Doing something to take care of myself wasn't a right that I had; the voice instructed me to do something that would make me feel terrible instead. Every time I wanted to go eat—if I even *looked* at food—a battle would begin to rage in my own head. *You can't have that. Do you want to run another ten-miler? Put it down.* I listened every time.

I became obsessed with food, but I didn't eat it. I knew every single calorie count in every single piece of food. My brain was constantly working at a mile a minute, calculating the caloric impact of something as simple as salad. It was the first thing that popped in my head at the very sight of food—even if I wasn't the one eating it. My mind flooded with nutritional information (*30 calories per ounce, 8 grams of protein per 100 grams*). The more I knew and could add up, the more I wanted to know.

I would get books from the library, and look online to learn about even foods I wouldn't have dreamed of eating. I wasn't using the information for anything specific; I wasn't trying to build a diet plan or even share the information. I just needed to know how many calories were in everything. It had become my obsession to know every single detail about every single food item out there.

Those details triggered the voice even more. *800 calories. Absolutely not. You can't eat that much.* No matter how loud it got or how ridiculous the things it said, I never questioned it. I only kept listening. A thought as simple as, *"Carbs? Again?"* was enough to make me walk away from the food my body needed so badly. I continued to give the voice power over my life. I was feeding it, and as I did, it got hungrier and hungrier and stronger and stronger.

With my new field of expertise, the already short list of foods I was willing to eat became even shorter. There wasn't much that wasn't off-limits. It was starting to make it harder and harder to hang out with my friends and do the things that they (and basically every other healthy teenager) do. Weekends were the hardest. One of my buddies, Tom, had the sort of home setup every high school senior dreams of: a furnished basement with windows to the outside that were just big enough to accommodate cases of beer and parents who were willing to turn a blind eye. Every Friday we'd go to Tom's to party it up. I had a system in place for these parties: I'd grab a can of beer, go to the washroom, dump it, and refill the can with water. Then I'd sip on that the whole night.

There was just one problem with this setup. Because the window was open to make it easier to grab the beers, even in the middle of winter, I was too cold to stay down there. Inevitably, after about 30 minutes, I'd have to go upstairs to find a warmer room. I'd find my way to the kitchen, open up the fridge and grab the jar of low-cal salsa Tom's mom kept in there. Then I'd pop open the jar, grab a spoon, and eat bites of salsa while my friends were downstairs drinking beer.

And so I kept going on in this way. Continuing to restrict my food and upping my workouts. Once I started running long workouts on almost no food, I started dropping weight very quickly. It wasn't long before the layers of clothing stopped masking my weight loss. I was noticeably underweight, but I still didn't stop. I was taking my workout regimen and my restricted diet really seriously; I worked as hard to lose weight as I did to keep up in school.

Unfortunately, none of my school work was really paying off anymore. Every single day I would be studying until 3:00 a.m, but my grades were still suffering no matter how much work I put in. I couldn't figure out why I was falling behind. Nobody else was studying as hard as I was, certainly none of my friends (who were all gripped in the throes of Senioritis), but they were doing just as well as me if not better. I now realize that it's because they were getting nutrition into their brain, and I was not. At the time though, the voice in my head was telling me that it was another thing that I was doing wrong. *"Look at you,"* it said, *"you can't even remember what you read an hour ago."*

I couldn't process the information I was trying to study and was falling behind in class. I was going to the gym, exercising all the time, and I was skipping dinner with my family every night, telling my parents that I had already eaten before they got home. Somehow it never occurred to me that my parents would take notice of my new routines and my increasingly gaunt appearance.

That all came to a head on my birthday. My mom planned to surprise me with a birthday cake she'd made using the lightest possible ingredients: angel food cake with fresh strawberries. She knew I wouldn't eat a heavy cake slathered in frosting and topped with ice cream. That night, she had invited my aunt, uncle, and cousin over for dinner to celebrate.

She had been visibly disappointed when I informed everyone that I had already eaten dinner on my way home from school and was no longer hungry. "But I told you yesterday *and* this morning not to eat ahead of time because I was inviting everyone over."

"Yeah, I'm sorry, Mom. I forgot." She shook her head as I put the plate she had set on the table for me back into the cupboard. I took my seat at the table and gave the rest of the family the same story that I had given my mom.

When dinner was over, I stood up to help clear the dishes. "No, no, Pete. You sit right back down," my mom said. "We've still got your cake."

"Oh, that's okay. We don't need to." It was all I could muster. I didn't know she had made me one.

"Just a small piece," she said as she lit the candle she had placed in the center.

"No."

"Pete," she said firmly, "it's your birthday."

"No."

"Knock it off, Pete. Your mom made you a birthday cake. You're being rude."

I looked back at my mom. I could see that she was upset. The last thing I wanted to do was hurt her feelings, but the voice in my head wouldn't stop. *Cake? Do you have any idea how much sugar is in that thing? You can't have that.* It was such a strong fear at that point. Every calorie was a battle, and even though I knew I was making my mom sad, I gave into the voice.

"I'm still full from eating dinner. I'll have a slice later."

I glanced over at my aunt, uncle, and cousin. I could tell by the look on their faces that they realized how bad it was. I didn't care that they knew or what they might think. I was so preoccupied with what was going on between my ears. Without another word to anyone, I turned and walked out of the room. My mom was still standing in the middle of the kitchen, holding my cake. My birthday candle had begun to drip wax on it.

I could hear my mom try to smooth it over as I walked up the stairs. She never liked to bother people or seek help if she doesn't have to. Instead, her M.O. was to carry on as though nothing was wrong and keep everyone feeling as comfortable as possible. I had no doubt that she would slice up the cake, pour coffee for everyone still at the table, and try to carry on pleasant conversation.

A few days later, I was walking through the kitchen after my parents had finished their dinner when my mom called me over to the table. "Pete, can you come sit with me for a minute?"

"Sure," I said as I moved into the chair next to her. My heart slowed as I did. It hadn't occurred to me before that she might know exactly what I was doing, but it certainly was now. I knew what she wanted to talk about.

She glanced quickly toward the living room, where my father was sitting on the couch watching TV, then reached into a bag she had propped against the table leg. She pulled out a book and quickly slid it over to me. "It's about eating disorders, honey, and what they can do to you." She bit her lip and looked like she was fighting to keep her composure as she said, "I know you haven't been eating."

I had been so focused on myself and on restricting that I didn't realize she had seen as much as she had. I thought I had done a good job of being discreet and covering up my eating. I had gone as far as trying to trick them. Every time I came home from school to find that my parents weren't home yet, or if

I knew they were still at work, I would make dinner for the family. I'd cook enough food for my parents and then I'd take one plate and smear some sauce or some leftover pieces on it. Then when they got home I'd set the plate in the sink and tell them, "Oh, dinner is ready. I was hungry so I ate already. Just finished." My mom might have fallen for it a time or two, but now I knew she saw right through me.

She pointed to a page that outlined the symptoms, showing me that they were all exactly what I had been doing. "Peter," she said (she rarely called me that), "you really can't continue doing what you are doing."

I looked at my mom, her face pleading but not judging. I looked back down at the book, which I knew on a logical level fit me to a tee, and I realized, "*I totally agree.*" I absolutely agreed with everything that she told me. "Okay, Mom, I'll try to make a change," I said, and I meant it.

Everything that I read and that my mom had said to me made perfect logical sense. And as I stood up from the table, my mind wasn't denying any of it. I told myself, "Okay. Tomorrow we're going to start fresh. We're going to make a change, and we're going to start over and start recovering." But unfortunately that mind of yours, that voice that develops inside your head, is pretty powerful, and it doesn't let you do what you want to do. It does what *it* wants to do, and it takes your body with it. The voice in my head was still controlling me whether I liked it or not, and logical arguments—even my own beliefs—weren't about to make it go away.

Of course, when that next day came, I restricted my food and overworked my body just as I had the day before. I walked into the house that evening, fresh out of the gym, and caught my mom's eye as she was setting a place for me at the table. She held up one of the plates as if to say, "Today?" I shook my head no and turned toward my bedroom. She frowned and set the plate down anyway. I walked back toward my room repeating the exact thought I had the night before. "Okay, tomorrow we're going to start again. Tomorrow we're going to start again."

And I dragged on this way for months, until I was finally hospitalized for anorexia. It was December 20th, 2002, just a few weeks after my birthday.

CHAPTER 3

ANOREXIA

I woke up in the hospital. My eyes were bleary at first, taking in the white walls and the white coat on the man standing to my right, who was jotting something down on a clipboard. Then I looked down and saw the IV in my arm, the heart monitor beside me beeping out a slow rhythm. I saw the tray of food being set down in front of me by a nurse in blue scrubs. "Try to eat this, Peter, if you can." Then I saw my mom standing behind her with the slick of tears creeping into her eyes.

What happened?

Earlier that day, my mom had stopped me from leaving for school. "Pete, I made you an appointment with the doctor. *A different doctor*," she added quickly. She told me how scared she was for me, how desperately she wanted me to go to this appointment. It had been months since she had given me the book on eating disorders, months since I had told her that I would make a change. And in those months, I had continued to restrict my eating and exhaust my body and had somehow continued to lose even more weight.

"I can't force you to go," she said as tears slid down her face, "and I won't. But I'm really hoping you'll come with me this morning."

I had made my mom cry, and it wasn't even 9:00 a.m. yet. I agreed to go. "Okay, okay, stop worrying. We'll go to the doctor, and we'll talk."

Now I couldn't remember much from the appointment. I definitely couldn't remember how I got to the hospital. "Mom," I croaked. My mouth was dry, my voice hoarse. She sat down next to me and handed me the cup of water that was sitting on my tray.

She didn't make me ask, but instead started talking as I drank.

"The doctor wasn't in the room for more than five minutes before he told me to take you to the Emergency room. He took your blood pressure, looked over at me and told us to go. I looked over at you and knew he was right. Your face had paled in just the time since we left the house."

"You said, 'Okay, let's go,' right?" I asked. It was coming back to me a little. I remembered that I didn't want to do it. "Did you talk me into going?"

"I thought I was going to have to. You started shaking your head, but then you stood up and started walking with me.

You didn't put up a fight at all. You just seemed...tired." She continued telling me about how lethargic I was on the drive over and how she couldn't tell if I was awake or asleep. "Do you remember any part of the drive?" she asked.

I shook my head. I had either blacked out or passed out—I had no idea which. And now I was here. I looked down at the food the nurse had set down in front of me: a roll—*carbs*; butter—*fat*; and a small bowl of Jello—*sugar*. I was terrified of it.

But at the same time, I felt relieved to be in a hospital bed. The last half-year of food restriction and heavy exercise had been extremely exhausting and mentally tiring. I knew that I had been hurting myself, but I somehow kept managing to push the thought away as I carried out my routines. Now there was a part of me that was thinking, "Wow! Okay! I am finally here. I am finally where I need to be." The other part couldn't stop staring at the food in front of me, trying to devise ways to not eat it. I was having very conflicting thoughts inside my head as I oscillated between, "Yes, I need to be here," and, "Why the hell am I here? I'm totally fine."

It had taken a long time to reach this point. My mom had tried to get me to the doctor plenty of times, and I'd always refuse. I'd tell her, "I'm busy. I'm too busy for a doctor. I've got school." I'd make up excuses and then force myself to sit down and eat with my family (still just very small portions) to try to ease her mind. She didn't want to be too pushy, too confrontational. But now that we were sitting in my hospital room, she wasn't holding back. She told me about how she could see the weight falling off of me, how pale I would get by the end of the day, and how quickly she suspected what was actually going on.

"I started talking to some of my friends about how scared I felt," she said. "Not a lot of people, just Susan and Colleen. They told me I was being silly." Her friends had chalked it up to growing pains. "He is a boy. He is growing up. Obviously is going to lose some baby weight as he gets older," and, "Kids' metabolism changes." They couldn't conceive that a boy—a high school senior—could be struggling with an eating disorder. Now I was in the hospital due to my anorexia.

"You knew though, huh?" I asked, feeling embarrassed.

"Yeah, baby, I did," she said. "Every mom knows her kid."

CHAPTER 4

SNEAKING AROUND

I spent six weeks in the hospital before I checked myself out. Staying there for that long was one of the hardest things I had ever done. I had to eat six meals a day and each meal had to be supervised. Someone was always watching to make sure that I ate everything I was given. I could take in only liquid food in the beginning. It took three or four days before I could start eating solids. My body was so malnourished that real food just wouldn't help me at that point. I needed to replenish what was lost in my body first.

It seemed that everything I did in the hospital was measured or weighed. In fact, taking my weight was the first thing I did each morning. The minute I woke up, I was walked over to a scale and my bodyweight was written down on a chart. When I went to pee, they'd measure how much I was peeing and write it down. My meal portions were meticulously measured, and at times I wondered whether they were writing down how many times I chewed each bite.

It was really uncomfortable for me to feel so exposed, but compared to some of the others in the hospital with me, I supposed I was one of their happier cases. There were people in there being treated for eating disorders who were also mentally ill or borderline suicidal. Some of the rooms had to be cleared of everything but the furniture just so they couldn't hurt themselves. I also couldn't help but notice that I was the only male in the entire facility where I was hospitalized. Every other patient around me was female. "Does this not happen to guys?" I remember thinking, "or do guys just never get help for eating disorders?" It was hard to tell for sure, and to this day, I don't think I know the answer, though I lean more toward the latter.

Some days it felt like I could very easily slip into despair with some of the others—not to the point that I would need the sharp objects pulled out of my room, thankfully, but there were some really bad days. Slowly, though, my mind started to shift. I eventually started telling myself, "I can get over this on my own. I see what I did wrong, and I know how not to repeat it."

I had a dream that I wanted to work for NASA one day; I wanted to go to university and get into aerospace, which meant I needed to get back to work. Once I started putting a plan back together, it got harder and harder to stay where I was. I ruminated on the time I was losing while staying in the facility.

One afternoon, I was so deep in thought that I didn't even notice when one of the nurses walked into my room.

"You're thinking hard," she said, pulling the corner of my bed sheet taut before walking over to the TV I forgot I had turned on. "Are you even watching this?"

I looked over at the soap opera on the screen, where everyone was confused about who the evil twin *really* was. "No. No, definitely not. I guessed I zoned out."

"I'll say. The one on the left is the evil one, by the way. You can tell by her eyeliner. In case you were wondering," she said with a wink. "So, what has you so thoughtful today?"

"School. About how I need to take my education and my schooling seriously, which means I need to get out of this hospital and go to school and do just that—school—and not to think about this eating disorder and start eating." I looked over at her and smiled because I probably sounded like I had a screw loose.

She smiled back at me, "All in good time, Peter. You'll get there and do all of that when you're ready. I'll leave you to your thinking anyhow, unless you want me to turn the soap opera back on." She signed off on a clipboard and started to walk out the room when I called after her.

"By the way, who decides when I get to leave this place anyway?"

It turned out that I was the one who got to make that call. My eighteenth birthday had come and gone, and, since I was technically an adult, I could check myself out of the hospital whenever I was decided to. It was all I could do to not race to the facility director's office in a full sprint. Nobody seemed particularly impressed with the idea. My doctors urged me not to leave, "You're not ready to check out just yet. Let the program run its course; it's only been six weeks."

No way. "No, I am ready," I responded. "I am ready to go home."

So, I left the hospital and set out to start on the plan I had concocted over the last few weeks. And what do you know? I was not ready.

For six months after that, I was caught up in what felt like a rollercoaster of results and failed progress—a twisted rollercoaster that never went any higher than base, just level down, up to base, level down, level down, up to base. I would gain a pound, I would lose a pound, gain a pound, lose four pounds. I would go into the hospital every two weeks for weigh-ins, and there'd be times right before the visit when I knew that I hadn't eaten enough that week. My solution? I would drink a bunch of water just to weigh up.

I'd pull into the parking lot with a few minutes to spare and proceed to chug almost a liter of water as fast as I could before walking into the hospital. It wasn't the easiest thing in the world to do, but it sounded a hell of a lot better than having to admit that I hadn't eaten as much as I was supposed to. The plan failed every time though; I would always come in underweight for some reason and then have to swear that I'd do better the next week. My water-chugging attempts were still a regular thing, though, in spite of all my promises to do better.

Little by little, I did start eating more here and there. I also started working out here and there, even though it was strictly against my doctor's orders. Before I checked out, he made it clear to me and to my parents that I wasn't supposed to be exercising. My parents, though they couldn't do anything to stop me from checking out of the facility, were not happy about my decision to leave. Therefore, they committed to these instructions.

As we drove home the day I left, my mom made it clear that I was to play by all the doctor's rules, and she put special emphasis on one. "You're not allowed to work out." I agreed at the time, but it didn't take long for me to break that promise.

One morning, I woke up feeling wide-awake even though it was still dark outside. I checked the clock by my bed. 5:25 a.m. The house was completely quiet, and I knew it would stay that way until my parent's alarm went off at 6:45.

Now's the time. I sat up, climbed out of bed, and silently made my way downstairs to the basement. I flipped the light switch and saw my weights and bench were exactly where I had left them. "Yes!" I whispered to myself and immediately launched into a set. These secret morning workouts became my new M.O. I would get up before six in the morning and go to the basement to work out quietly with weights. This furtive, underground training was the only way I thought I could recover.

After my roller coaster six months had passed, I broached the idea of going back to the gym to my mom. I figured it was a matter of time before she or my father woke up early enough to catch me in the basement anyway. "Mom, I want to work out," I said, doing my best to make my tone strike a balance between "please let me" and "please don't force me to do this behind your back, because I will."

She gave me one of her looks, the kind that made me pretty sure she could see right through me, and said, "All right, all right, you can work out. Go do your thing. If that's what's going to make you happy, then do it." The smile she gave me afterward let on that she either knew that I was already sneaking in my workouts, or that I could have asked for it weeks ago.

Once I was working out again, I wanted to eat a lot. Or at least my body did. I was still very mentally screwed up and grappled with a fear of food that I couldn't shake. I wanted to eat—I knew that I needed to eat—but mentally it was hard. I started looking into supplements as a way to even out the eating that I had to do against the potential weight gain that I feared.

The only problem was that I didn't have any money. My heart sank as I walked past aisle after aisle of carb blockers, fat blockers, fat burners, and metabolism boosters, all boasting price tags that would obliterate the meager stack of cash in my bank account.

Then I saw my saving grace tucked in the back of the store, like a beacon glowing amidst a stormy sea: the clearance section. I turned over a few bottles. There, underneath a printed expiration date that had already come and gone, was a sticker that read "99 cents". I glanced back at the expiration date—it was only past by a week or so. "I'm sure it's still effective," I thought and started scooping up as many kinds as I saw, stocking up on a little bit of everything.

Every time I ate a lot of food, I would just take a bunch of these pills to help ease my mind in thinking, "Okay, I'll be fine now. I won't get fat," or "I won't gain that much weight from what I just ate. I won't gain too quickly."

I knew my mom would flip out if she knew I was taking fat- and carb-blockers at all, let alone *expired* fat- and carb-blockers. So, I kept them hidden in a CD player case. At one point, I actually filled the whole case up with different pills, with nothing else inside. I carried it around everywhere but never made attempt to look like I wanted to listen to it.

The stakes got a little higher when my mom and I were en route to Poland on a trip to visit her family. Our plane had been in the air for a little over an hour, and I could see that dinner service was about to get started. I casually reached into my bag to grab some blockers before the airline attendants came around with their vacuum-sealed dinners. I slid the pill into my mouth, closed the case, re-zipped the bag, and sat up in a single fluid motion. (I had gotten very good at this.) But when I sat up, I saw my mom staring right at me from across the plane aisle.

She looked at me intensely and with a quick flick of her head told me to meet her in the middle of the plane at the bathrooms. I sighed, unclipped my seatbelt, and started to stand up. "Bring whatever is in your bag," I heard her say as she stood up and started walking back. I grabbed the CD player and followed her to the bathrooms.

As soon as I reached the bulkhead, she asked me, "What are they?"

"Supplements," I said, "some vitamins and protein too."

"Can I see them?"

I handed her the CD player case. She popped it open and nearly had to slam it shut to keep my stash of pills from falling out. "Where did you get all these?" she asked. "*How did you afford them?*"

I wasn't about to fess up to taking expired pills, so I just replied, "I found them for a good price. It's not like I spent hundreds of dollars or anything."

She looked away from me for a moment and handed the bag back. "You've got to stop taking these pills."

I was defeated, and I knew it. "Yeah, you're probably right. I probably need to." And I agreed to dump them all. It was actually really, really hard to do because I knew I wouldn't have anything to turn to for the next couple weeks we were in Poland. Even if I did try to buy supplements there, I'd have no idea where to find them or even what to look for.

For the next two weeks, I was eating without the assistance of any blockers, burners, or shredders—my mental crutch. It was difficult, but I also felt a lot more at ease as the trip went by. It felt good to be with my family, to focus on something other than what I was putting into (and trying to keep out of) my body.

So, it was the first step, I guess, to starting recovery.

CHAPTER 5

RECOVERY

After convincing me to ditch the supplements I had been carrying around with me, my mom did everything she could to support me during out trip to Poland. She helped me with trying to eat as clean, lean, and healthy as possible—something that was often easier said than done in Krakow, particularly when we were visiting my grandparents' house. Each time we came over, they would serve heavy cake and pastries. It was old world European hospitality at it's finest, and, even though I was feeling a little better, I couldn't bring myself to even consider taking a piece. Not even when it was on a plate held in my grandmother's outstretched hand.

"We had lunch before we came," I stammered as I held up my hand and slightly backed away.

"That's right," I heard my mom say behind me. "Ice cream too. Thanks, but I don't think we could manage another dessert."

She backed me up, and she would do so again and again throughout the trip.

There were a lot of questions as to why I was in the hospital. We didn't sit down and explain it. Old school Polish grandparents don't understand eating disorders, and my mom and I weren't about to offer an in-depth explanation. My mom wrangled the conversation like a pro. She offered a vague reason—"He was ill, but he is doing much better now."—and steered discussion in a new direction.

When we were packing and getting ready to catch our flight home, I leaned over toward her. I wanted to say something that could eloquently sum up how much gratitude I felt for her on this trip. The best I could muster was, "Mom. Thanks..."

She gave me a hug and responded, "Of course, honey. All that mattered to me on this trip was for you to be clear and not worried about this stuff. I was willing to do whatever it took, and that's not going to change just because we're heading back home.

I came back from Poland in a much better headspace than the one I had left with. It was difficult initially to not dive directly back into what I had been doing—monitoring my food intake, over-exercising, replenishing my eradicated supplement stores—but this time I was truly determined not to. I told myself, "Okay, so we stop that. Now it's time to figure everything else out. Figure out the rest of my life." It was September 2003; 18 months after a misdiagnosis threw my world down the spiral.

I felt more at ease because I didn't have to think about taking a handful of pills after every single time I ate. I was still very careful about what I was eating—but I was eating—and in that way was exercising control without relying on anything but myself. It was just one very small bit of the puzzle, of course, but it made a difference. And I came back from our trip to Poland feeling very determined to move forward.

I refocused my attention on my schooling. I had passed high school, luckily, but with grades that didn't get me into the universities I wanted. So, I went back to high school for a year to boost my grades. I also thought it was a good idea considering everything that happened—maybe I wasn't ready for university yet.

So during this time, I was only taking a few classes, and with that extra time on my hands, I started thinking that it was the right time for me to dedicate myself to doing whatever it took to get better. The only hard part was that I wasn't sure what that was. I had to figure it out as time went on.

In September of 2003, I signed up to a fitness forum, and I decided that I was going to start sharing what was going on in my life. During the months after I left the hospital, I had received nothing but support from my family members. They were telling me that I was doing a good job and that things will be better. My mom was always quick to tell me, "You don't need to be afraid of gaining weight because you're going to be fine," and quick to tell me how loved I was. It was great, of course, to receive that kind of encouragement from her, but hearing something from your family is a lot different than hearing it from someone who doesn't know you.

When encouragement or advice comes from someone objective, it carries more weight—at least, it does to me. And in that way, the online fitness forums were a huge factor in my recovery. The outside opinions that came to me through the different message boards were much more impactful and more effective in spurring me along in my efforts. I started to engage more and more with the community on the site. I posted pictures of my progress; I posted my story, my diet, and my training to a bodybuilding.com forum under the screen name "dedicated for life".

The name was one that immediately really resonated with me. I wanted to stick with my recovery and pursue a transformation, to dedicate myself to a lifestyle that was truly healthy. I had seen countless transformations in different magazines, and I finally reached the point where I was thinking, "Why can't I do it?" The more I started reading about healthy, balanced diets, about training, and about other people's success stories, the more I started to believe that I could make the same positive changes in my own life. "Dedicated for life" gave me my banner.

I started to eat more. I started working out in a way that wasn't about tearing down my body. I started going out more with friends during this time, which was a hugely positive shift. I hadn't realized it before, but as I was locked in my obsession with restriction and exercise, I was also extraordinarily lonely. Trying to keep my restrictions, my workouts, my supplements, and even the thoughts running through my head a secret had led to me almost completely cutting myself off from the people I cared about. I may have been physically present in the room with them from time to time, but I wasn't connecting with them. I was too busy trying to hide what was going on in my life. I would have never dreamed a year earlier that I would now be telling both friends and strangers the truth about what I had been doing. The first year I spent being "dedicated for life" was a big struggle, but it was also big success since I actually put on some weight. When I look at progress pictures from 2003 to 2004, there's a huge difference. (Note: These and other photos are at the end of the book.)

Then came the opportunity to share my story on a much larger scale.

The owner of bodybuilding.com contacted me saying, "You're an incredible transformation. You're doing awesome. Can you write an article about what you're doing so far?" As far as external motivation and encouragement goes, I didn't think it could get any bigger for me. His message pushed me to think, "Yeah, I am doing great. I am making real progress. I've got to keep this going." So I did, day after day. And I also kept sharing.

While I was making progress mentally and physically, my transformation wasn't quick, and it wasn't smooth. During this time (in fact, for three and half years after leaving the hospital), I would still grapple with the voice inside of my head telling me the different negative things that I had become so used to: that people around me were judging me and that

I needed to keep restricting food. It happened all the time, especially at the start.

I would make a gain of some kind, and, like clockwork, the voice would try to hinder me. It felt like my brain would get hijacked as I caught myself starting to listen and believe what it was saying again. It sometimes got so intense that I would scream at the voice to get the hell out and leave me alone. I would yell at myself in the mirror, "You're better than this!" I did everything I could to steel myself mentally and keep going. I was constantly reminding myself, "I'm allowed to eat. People don't think I'm an idiot. I want to get better. You're killing yourself, Pete. You're better than this."

I would try to motivate myself rather than fight the voice. As I progressed with my fitness, improved my relationship with food, and became more comfortable with my body image and eating, the voice got quieter.

But I found that the more I talked to other people through the forums, the videos I posted, and then later through the articles I wrote, the more this voice started to fade away, slowly but surely. It took a very long time (and there was a lot of yelling out to myself during that time), but over time. I wasn't hearing what I was hearing before.

I'm sure that other people probably thought I was recovered before I actually had. I was already putting on weight, and I looked much healthier. But it was the mental component of my recovery that was the most meaningful and important to me. It wasn't about my weight or physique. It was about what was going on in my head. The biggest lesson that came out of my eating disorder and recovery is that everything comes down to what you're thinking mentally; if you're thinking negatively all the time, then you can't live life happily.

My mentality became another component of "dedicated for life." It became something I valued, prioritized, and protected. As I did, the hold my old habits had on me started to fall away just as the voice inside my head had. Years before, when I was looking at food, I would still try to process calories or I would think about the amount of protein and carbohydrates I was taking in. Now, I wasn't thinking about it as much, and if I did, it was no longer bothering me the way that it had.

Which is how I eventually found myself sitting in a greasy spoon diner in 2007 ready to take down the biggest breakfast of my life.

CHAPTER 6

THE LINEBACKER

It was early 2007. I was in my third-year at university at the time, and, like any self-respecting upperclassman, I had spent the previous night out at the bars with my friends. We had gone out on a pub-crawl the night before and had partied it up hard. We all got pretty smashed, drank quite a bit, and woke up feeling broken, battered, and smelling like a distillery. "Ugh," my buddy Mike said as he walked into the common room. "My mouth tastes like cardboard...and cats. Breakfast. Now."

One of the most popular places in the city was this place called Christina's Pub. They served all the typical greasy breakfast dishes. Breakfast was just what they were known for. And if you were five extremely hung-over guys, there was no other place in town that could fix you better than Christina's. They even had this dish called the Linebacker. Now, on this Linebacker plate was every breakfast item you could ever think of—in fact, there were *two* of every single breakfast item. So you had bacon, you had ham, you had French toast, you had pancakes, you had regular toast, you had eggs, and you had hash browns. The dish was so big that you didn't usually see anybody but big football players come in and order it. And a lot of the time even they could barely eat it. It's a lot of food, but that morning, man, it was the only thing I wanted. With extra bacon. I was that hung over.

I dug in as soon as our plates hit the table. The other guys had only ordered eggs or waffles and a few sausage links, but I still managed to finish my plate before anyone else had finished even a quarter of theirs.

Mike looked over at me and almost dropped his fork. "Whoa, whoa, whoa, whoa, *whoa*. What are you doing? That was really fast."

I looked down at my empty plate. "I was just...I don't know...I was hungry. I just wanted to kill this hangover."

Mike grinned at me and started laughing. Then he reached for his wallet. There are few things he loves more than to challenge his friends to do random things. It's one of his true passions. So when the waitress came back, he asked her, "Hey, what's the record for the most of those Linebacker plates eaten at one time? Is there even a record?" "Oh, I don't think we've kept track of records or anything like that," she said.

"Okay, fine," Mike said. "Who ate the most then?"

"Well, somebody once ate two of these in one hour. I guess that's the record."

"Perfect," Mike said, looking straight at me.

When she walked away, he slapped two twenties on the table. "If you beat this record, I'll give you $40 and pay for your entire bill."

"You know these things are like $10 a plate, right?"

"Yep."

"Okay," I replied, "Sounds good, let's do it up."

Mike turned his head over his shoulder. "Waitress!"

They brought me two Linebacker dishes maybe ten minutes later. I managed to polish off everything on those two plates in about five minutes. We all glanced around the table at each other as if to say, "Wow, we still have some time."

Mike looked down at his empty mug of coffee. "I could go for a refill. How about you, Pete?"

So they ordered up one more Linebacker breakfast, and I managed to polish that one off as well. And, truth be told, I could have kept on going, but I already felt like a pig. And with the carb hangover definitely setting in, I decided to just call it a day and happily took Mike's money.

As we walked out, my buddy Rik slapped me on the back and laughed. "I guess they've got an official record now."

"8 eggs, 8 strips of bacon, 8 sausage, 8 scoops of home fries, 8 pancakes, 8 French toast, and 8 regular toast in less than an hour," our friend Ramy added.

"Dude, really though," Rik said. "Where did that come from? Have you started doing eating contests or something?"

"No," I replied. "It's not like that's a regular breakfast order for me or anything. This was a special occasion. I'd never pass up a chance to take Mike's money."

"Oh, ha," Mike chimed in.

"Seriously though," Rik continued, "how'd you pull it off?"

I shrugged. "I guess I can eat."

CHAPTER 7

NUGGETS, BAGELS, AND OATS

The Linebacker challenge had been a big joke among my friends and me, and in the days after, we would laugh about finding more challenges for me to take on.

I started looking around for other restaurant challenges and found that there weren't very many out by the university. So, I switched my search over to the Internet and started doing some challenges online. The best online challenges were actually on bodybuilding.com, the same site where I was posting my story in the fitness forums.

Within these forums, you have conversations about training, about nutrition, and then you have a company promotion section. Within the company promotions section were all of these online eating challenge contests. Each were sponsored and hosted by a different company. The way it worked was simple: you recorded yourself eating as much as you possibly could—it could be anything—in a two-minute time frame. And whoever ate the most in that time frame would win, say, $100 worth of free supplements from the host company. I had been aware of them for years, but I never thought to actually *do* one. Now I couldn't get enough of them. Armed with a $5 webcam that was about as high-tech as a potato, I took on every challenge that came my way.

I won a Bagel Bites challenge (35 in two minutes) and tackled 1500 grams of cooked oats. This challenge took a bit of strategizing. Eat it all at once and I'd be stuck with the equivalent of drying concrete before I was even halfway through my bowl. So, I broke it into three 500-gram segments, which made the challenge logistically easier but much tougher on the ol' psyche. I had to dress up the final 500 grams with maple syrup, almonds, and raisins to get the job done and even then it was a struggle to reach the bottom of the bowl. Oats and I had a falling out that day, but I still won the challenge. In fact, I won every challenge I entered.

Except one.

The chicken nugget challenge. It was a simple one: eat as many chicken nuggets as you can in two minutes. I scoped out the competitors that had already posted their videos. The guy on the top of the leaderboard had eaten 18 in two minutes. "All right, all right," I thought. "18 is easy." There were still two days left in the competition though. I figured I should play it safe and put a little distance between my score and the rest of the pack.

"So in order to clean up the competition, I'm going to eat 30 of them as fast as I can," I said into the camera. Then I hit the start button on my stopwatch and went to town on my 30 pieces of chicken. I annihilated the pile, but I did it in less than 90 seconds, leaving myself 30 extra seconds of eating time. The problem was that I was out of nuggets. I had only planned for, bought, and prepared 30. Since I was out of chicken, I had no choice but to stop. And that's how I lost. Some guy ended up winning with the 31 pieces he was able to eat in the full two-minute time allotment. It was my first and last online challenge loss.

Other than that, I won every single one, and it was rarely ever a close victory. I just crushed everyone. It got to the point that people started getting really pissed off about it and started dropping comments on the challenge pages saying, "All right, so I'm going for second place again," every single time. Fortunately for me, the majority of the people on the site rallied around me and were supportive of me and kept the competitions fun.

The community support on bodybuilding.com was (and still is) awesome. In fact, it was a big part of what drew me into the site's forums back when I started my road to recovery in September 2003. Back when I told myself, "It's time to turn around," and declared myself "dedicated for life." The transformation that had brought me to this point was the kind of decision only I could make for myself, and when I did. it was the support of the online community that pushed me through my toughest days. Now the community was supporting me as I discovered my ridiculous new talent. My friends offline were more than happy to find challenges for me too. They thought it was hilarious. And while they were thoroughly entertained by my goofy videos, they wanted to see how my eating skills fared in the real world.

My friends and I decided it was time to take my talents out into Toronto.

LONE STAR TEXAS GRILL

Challenge: Finish a 72-Ounce
Steak + Side in under 1 hour

{ 12 MINUTES }

What kinds of challenges are out there? My friends and I started looking around Toronto and neighboring cities and towns for other ways to test my eating speed. It didn't take long before we sat down in front of one of the better-known challenges in the area: the 72-ounce steak at the Lone Star Texas Grill.

The Lone Star's challenge was to eat an entire 72-ounce steak and a side in under one hour. If you could finish it in time, the steak was free. If you couldn't, you had to pay for it. I was psyched to tackle the steak. It was the most popular running record we had been able to find in our hunt for eating challenges. It was the one people talked about the most, which is saying something because "Man versus Food" (or anything like it) didn't exist yet. In fact, competitive eating in general just wasn't really talked about. It wasn't really common at all. On top of all that, this was going to be the biggest amount of food I'd ever tried to eat and definitely the biggest piece of meat I'd ever seen in my life, and I was really excited to see if I could do it.

Apparently there were only two people who had ever accomplished the feat before at this specific location, and the record times, 58 minutes and 45 minutes respectively, sounded beatable to me. I had an hour to finish my steak, but obviously wanted to try to break the standing records.

Two of my friends, Mike and Adrian, came with me, and we decided to actually make a lunch of it, rather than just make the trip all about the challenge. My buddies ordered their lunches—something sensible, a chicken caesar salad and a burger—and all of our plates came out together. After setting down our lunches, our waitress glanced my way and said, "Well, good luck. You have an hour."

I started eating at a slow pace because the meat was just a few degrees less than the surface of the sun—in other words, I hadn't started trying yet. But when our waitress came back after about a minute, she looked at the 1.5 bites I had taken and visibly checked out. I'm sure she was thinking, "All right, great. He's probably not going to finish it." She spun on her heel and made her way to the back for a smoke break, assuming, "These guys will be busy for a bit. I've got time."

So, I kept casually eating this steak. After all, my friends were enjoying their meals and I didn't want to them to feel rushed. We were laughing about it as I made my way through.

"I think you should eat the fat first. Just to make a statement," Mike said as I finished the first ten percent in about two minutes.

I looked at him mid-bite. "I will," and sliced off a hunk of fat, popped it in my mouth and smiled at him.

"Oh, you're definitely going to make it under the 20-minute mark."

"Dude, you're going to finish your lunch before I do."

"I don't know, man. I've still got the chewy part."

The center of the steak had to have been at least three inches thick. The thickness coupled with the fact that I had ordered it cooked rare made for some extremely chewy steak. Plus, with only about 4 ounces to go, I was starting to get full. And there was still the side: a plate of shoestring potato salad. I picked up the pace a little just to make sure I didn't get too full too fast.

I finished my entire 72-ounce steak along with the side in 12 minutes. And I didn't really try. My buddies and I were actually kind of surprised at the time because I wasn't going for speed—I was just eating. I think everyone else around us was shocked though. Management came out to congratulate us, telling us that I had probably beaten the top record for all

Lone Star locations. "I think the longest-standing record was just over 20 minutes," he said. Our waitress hadn't come back in from her smoke break yet.

We paid our bill with the manager and walked out to the car. "You gave up, huh?" We heard a voice call out from behind us, "That's too bad." We turned and saw our waitress standing by the corner of the building, assuming I had given up and left when my buddies were done with their lunch.

"Nah," Mike said, "He totally crushed it."

She looked at me, "You mean you're already done? And you *finished it?*" She was definitely shocked.

"The side too," Mike added, "and we left your cash on the table." We started laughing about the stunned look on her face as she listened to Mike's comments. She just really couldn't believe it.

We turned and kept walking toward the car.

"Was the steak good though?" Adrian asked me. "It looked good."

"Yeah, it was good," I said, "but I wouldn't want to pay for it."

"It was, what, $45.00?" Mike asked.

"Yep," I replied. "I'd rather just eat it fast."

Mike shrugged. "It really is a good value though."

CHAPTER 9

TEXAS LONGHORN

Challenge: Finish a 106-Ounce
Steak + baked potato and a
salad in 106 minutes

{ 30 MINUTES }

After smashing the record at Lone Star, shocking their staff, and appalling their customers, I actually went for a bigger meat challenge at another place called Texas Longhorn just a few days later. I guess you could say I was going through a little bit of a steak phase.

Their challenge was a little different. You weren't competing against yourself, trying to finish your huge steak in an hour; you were competing against the standing in-house record time—and you were given a one-minute-per-ounce time limit.

The house record was 105 ounces in 105 minutes, which mean that I had 106 minutes to finish my 106-ounce steak. And it came with a baked potato and a salad that had to be finished under my time as well.

This steak was a thick, terrible cut of meat. It came looking like a roast meant to feed a family of six. It was fatty and gristly—and it had been cooking for two hours. It was absolutely horrible. On the wall in front of my table were pictures of the previous record holders. The guy I was competing against, the one who ate 105 ounces in 105 minutes, looked like he was as wide as he was tall. It made sense, then, that my waitress looked at me like I didn't stand a chance as she handed me the waiver and a pen.

But I managed to destroy it in 30 minutes. I glanced over at my buddies. "Should I get dessert?"

"Obviously you should get dessert."

The manager brought over the dessert list and reminded me that I didn't have to eat any more to win the record. "Unless you want to."

"How about the cheesecake?"

"It's big," she said.

"Sounds good," I smiled and handed the dessert list back to her.

Damn it was a big piece of cheesecake though. The slice was

several inches tall and covered the entire width of the plate. "It's a good thing I love cheesecake," I said and took it down in four bites.

Then I looked over at my boss, who had decided to tag along with us. "Hey, Danny, I bet you don't get many interns who do this."

I had just started working in an internship for his company between my third and fourth year at university. I had only been there for about four months, but it was a small department filled with lots of buttoned-up physics people in lab coats making telescopes for the U.S. military—and then there was Danny and I. So in that short time, he and I had gotten to know each other a little bit.

I had told him the day before about my 72-ounce steak, and he was actually really interested in the story (or just entertained). So when I was leaving for the weekend, I popped my head into his office to tell him I was going to tackle the 106-ouncer.

"There's a 106-ounce steak at the Texas Longhorn. I'm going to go eat it."

"What the hell? When?"

"Now."

"Steak for happy hour, huh?"

I nodded my head. Without another word, he stood up,

grabbed his cell phone and wallet, and started walking out of his office. "I want to see this."

After I finished the steak and my dessert, we headed back out to the car. "So, Pete, I gotta know," Danny said, "which was harder to do? The steak or the cheesecake after the steak?"

"They were both fine," I said. "The steak cut was a little bit of a rough cut, otherwise it would've been a breeze."

"Well, yeah," he replied, "I can't imagine they're using their choicest pieces for things like this. That was cool though."

As rough as that steak/roast was, it wasn't the worst cut of meat I'd have to take down as part of an eating challenge.

I went back to the Lone Star a couple times to take on their 72-ounce steak. On the fourth visit, a newspaper came in to document the challenge. I don't know if it was the extra publicity that made Lone Star want to stack the deck, but I swear they gave me the worst cut of steak on this entire planet. In the prior challenges, they had always given me a nice cut, butterflied it, and seasoned it well. This time, though, they gave me an actual roast.

Our strategy for doing these Lone Star challenges was to never go to the same location twice. For one thing, we weren't even sure if we would be allowed to do it again if I was the standing record holder. We also figured that these restaurants never talked to one another, so if we went into a new location, they'd have no idea that I could smash their steak. My thought process was, "If I go somewhere else, no one will ever know, right?" I was wrong. This Lone Star knew about me in advance, and they had planned accordingly.

"*Ah, they are trying to screw with me,*" I thought as they set out the steak. "*They really just don't want me to finish this.*" The price tag for this challenge was well over the usual $45-for-failing. I was on the hook for $200 if I couldn't finish the steak, *and* there was a reporter there. It was clear that they were trying to make my life as difficult as possible.

I knew almost right away that I wasn't going to beat my time. Taking down this roast was going to be a mind over matter thing.

Gradually it became harder and harder to even force myself to slice off another bite. I had moved from using a knife and fork like a civilized human to essentially just stabbing and tearing at the meat. Then, with my eyes half-closed, would try to aim the bite at my face. I couldn't go on like this.

I didn't beat the record. There was no way I could possibly have beaten it with that kind of meat. I was pissed off afterward. I felt like they were purposefully trying to screw me. It was embarrassing with the reporter there and the crowd that had formed. But even that wasn't the worst steak challenge I had to take down.

After I had been competing professionally for about a year, I did a 76-ounce steak challenge with a piece of meat that could be best described only one way: a cow's ass. It's what it looked like, it's what it felt like, and it sure as hell is what it tasted like. It was just awful. After my first bite, I decided that I needed to destroy this thing as fast as possible and get out of there. I tried to keep chewing to a minimum so I didn't have to taste it too much.

As people watched me essentially throw chunks of meat down my throat, they were probably thinking, "How can anyone eat like this?"

I, on the other hand, was looking at the foulest piece of meat I had ever come across wondering, "How can anyone serve this?"

Despite the crowd and the reporter that had gathered for my failed Lone Star Steak Challenge, I wasn't doing this specifically to try to make a name for myself in the competitive eating sphere. Not even close. Even though I was winning my online challenges and starting to attract some attention for my eating, my first year of doing these contests, filming them, and posting them to the forums were basically me just making a joke out of this stuff. I really was not taking it seriously at all. I'd do online two-minute challenges, tackle local challenges, and still try to get Mike to put money on the line.

And I'd post my videos to YouTube.

My page consisted of some of my bodybuilding videos and every eating challenge I filmed. There were lots of those "most you can eat in two minutes" videos. There was an ice cream sandwiches video (8 in two minutes, then 16 in two minutes). There were hard-shelled tacos (9 in two minutes). I ate 40+

peanut butter and banana sandwiches with chocolate milk, which was too intense even for me. (Please, never do this.) I was basically eating anything that I thought would be funny and impress my friends. But as I was doing all this, I was actually gaining traction and popularity on those bodybuilding.com forums and on my YouTube page. A lot of people were talking about it and creating buzz. And they thought what I was doing was crazy and awesome and badass.

I thought it was funny that people were getting into something so goofy, but I kept posting and slowly kept getting more subscribers. Then I beat a World Record, and that changed everything.

CHAPTER 10

LONE STAR TEXAS GRILL

*Challenge: Finish a 72-Ounce
Steak + Side in under 1 hour*

{ UNDER 7 MINUTES }

"Hey, wanna try the 72-ounce steak again?" Mike asked me.

"Yeah, definitely." It had become a regular thing; something to do when our workload was light and we didn't have other plans.

We called ahead to a new Lone Star and made plans to go in the next day. "Why don't we make it interesting?" Mike said. "Look up what the World Record is."

If I were going to beat the record, I would have to finish the steak and the sides in less than 9 minutes and 28 seconds. I felt like I could do it, but in the back of my mind, I was also thinking, "Man, that's fast for that much steak." We were all stoked about the idea though, and the more we talked about it, the more I built up the can-do mindset that is so essential if you want to punish a huge piece of beef. "Yes, I'm going to do it." We were so busy rallying that we barely even noticed the blizzard happening outside our apartment.

The blizzard kept going the entire night and into the next day, dumping snow everywhere and basically shutting down the whole city. A normal person would have looked outside, looked at the road conditions, and said, "Nope. Not today." It was absolutely insane out there. But, for some stupid reason, we were determined to go. We kept pumping each other up, especially if it looked like someone was having a crisis of motivation, saying, "No, we're getting it done. We're going. We're going to go do this".

We drove downtown, which was normally a half an hour away, but with driving snow and barely visible roads, it took a little more than an hour and a half to get there. When we did finally get there, we walked into basically an empty restaurant. There was nobody there. We hadn't seen a soul out on the road as we drove in either.

I looked at Mike. "Nobody is downtown because nobody else was crazy enough to drive in that terrible, terrible weather."

"They don't have our fortitude," he replied.

It was just us and ten bored employees, and they were *ready* to serve us, glad to have something to do. Little did they know I wasn't going to be paying for my meal, because if you finish the 72-ounce steak in under an hour, you get it free of charge. This Lone Star, thankfully, hadn't heard anything about me.

We set up our camera. We start recording, and then we got the steak. The steak was a little overcooked, but after the roast I had last time, it was nothing I couldn't handle. I was psyched up and ready to go.

I ate the entire thing in just under seven minutes, breaking the standing World Record. Then I tackled two sides in another minute and a half to break that Lone Star's steak challenge record. And everyone around us—the bored wait staff and the two other tables that happened to walk in—was looking at each other like, "What the hell just happened?"

"Nice work!" the manager said, walking over. "Do you do this professionally or something?"

"No," I replied, "I just do it for fun."

"What else have you done this with?"

I shrugged. "Lots of steaks. Tacos, PB&J."

"God. How do you feel when you're done with something like this?" he asked, motioning to my empty plate.

"It depends on what I'm doing. With something like a straight meat product, actually you don't feel that bad. It's like the stuff that like spikes your insulin levels, like a lot of sugar or carbs or something creamy that starts turning in your stomach. That's the stuff that isn't so much fun, and you don't feel as great after that. But the meat stuff, you don't feel that bad. At least not until you start getting the meat sweats."

He laughed and shook my hand. We walked out of the Lone Star victorious once again.

Maybe it was the weather conditions, the record-breaking, or maybe it was just a slow news week, but that one event got a lot of media attention. I got a ton of calls from a lot of newspapers and radio stations, and I realized that a lot of people were talking about it. And then I got a call inviting me to my first eating competition in California.

CHAPTER 11

COLLEGIATE NATIONALS

After I broke the World Record for eating a 72-ounce steak, I got a call from a guy named Arnie who invited me out to California for an eating competition. "Dude, your records are unreal. You're going to be amazing." He told me more about the Collegiate Nationals in San Diego, California. "There are going to be crazy college eaters. Cash prizes if you win and the hotel is covered, everything."

I was sold. I told Arnie, "Sweet, this is awesome. Let's do it," and that was that. Signing up for Collegiate Nationals brought me a lot of media attention; the competition had a lot more drive around it than I realized. A nearly free trip to California was an easy sell to my buddies too. Mike, Jamie, and Gavin were all game for a trip out to San Diego (which is rarely a hard sell). We hopped on the plane and headed west.

It felt surreal driving through California on our way to an eating competition. I had heard about these kinds of contests before, but I guess I didn't really think they were real. Now, all of a sudden, they were not only real, but they had also comped us a rental car.

When we got to the contest, it was an awesome scene. There were a lot of heavy hitters there, a lot of people with crazy records—one guy ate 250 wings in a sitting and another guy had taken down 85 grilled cheese sandwiches—and people from all over the country had come out to compete. There was a huge crowd there to watch the events too. And it was all televised for CBS.

It was a *huge* departure from my usual eating challenges, which were performed in my living room in front of my video camera (now upgraded from the potato-cam to my dad's digital point and shoot). I had thought that the online response my videos had received was really cool, but this was on a whole other level, especially once my friends got the crowd to start chanting for me.

All of this made me extra nervous. I had set really low expectations for my performance in this competition—I guess it was out of intimidation more than anything else—but now I wanted to win. I told myself, "Okay, I know I'm good. I'm going to try my best, but I don't think I can beat these guys because they talk up a good game."

Instead of meeting my low expectations, I ended up crushing everybody. I ate 50% more food than the second placed person. I just destroyed everyone.

It was all college food—like a burger, a hot dog, and fries—all piled on to plates, and then our performance was measured by how many plates we finished. It definitely wasn't pleasant. It wasn't easy either. The food was pretty damn cold and dry, so it was actually a very slow eat. I only finished three and a half plates of food in seven minutes. But it was still double what my competitors were doing. I walked out of my first big competition at the top of the leaderboard.

"Pete the Professional Eater," Gavin said, slapping my back after I emerged victorious. "How does it feel to be in the big leagues?"

"I don't know," I replied. "The same?"

I remember noticing how serious some of the other competitors were about the challenges and their performance. My buddies and I were the exact opposite. We were just there to have a good time, party in San Diego, and ride this weird wave of opportunity that was coming my way.

CHAPTER 12

CHUG

Challenge: 1.5 Liters of Water in under 5 Seconds

As I started to gain more and more traction online, I started to focus a little more on delivering the kinds of videos other people might think were cool. There was a very, very popular video on YouTube featuring a Japanese guy drinking 1.5 liters of water in 4.88 seconds. It was insane. And it was also insanely popular. It had millions of views online. So I thought, "I've got to try that. I drink a lot of water on a regular basis anyway. I'm sure I can beat him. Or at least, I can come close."

Drinking 1.5 liters of water in under five seconds is as hard as it sounds. It took a couple tries, but I got better and better. And eventually I did a YouTube video in which I drank 1.5 liters of water in four and a half seconds. When I posted it, the response was nuts—tons of shares and tons of comments saying, "That's crazy," in some way, shape, or form. But it also brought me some of my first real haters.

When I filmed the video I did the challenge shirtless—after all, if something went weird with the challenge I would have ended up wearing all the water. And it just so happened that the shorts I was wearing actually created this funky crease that made it look like I was a little excited to do what I was doing, if you know that I mean. It was really noticeable too. So people made all these comments and remarks about it, and it got to me. I was pissed because I felt like I was being made fun of. It was embarrassing. But at that point my highest viewed video was probably like 5,000 views, while this video had nearly 300,000 views.

Still, I was so bothered by the comments that I said, "Screw this, I'm deleting this video." I pulled it from my site. In an instant, the video was gone forever. It was a snap decision that I still regret to this day.

Looking back, I hate that I let the negative comments get the better of me. I think about it now and wonder, "How did I delete that? *Why* did I delete that?" That decision ended up costing me money because I could safely say it would have close to 20 million at this point. I didn't realize it at the time, but I was taking money out of my own pocket because I let other people get under my skin.

It's crazy if you look back at it like that, but the online world is hard to take in. A lot of people don't understand how difficult it is to make videos and embrace the hate that is out there. Making a video and being excited about it and accepting all the comments and criticism that come in day in and day out becomes difficult sometimes, *especially* at the start. I had been so used to the positive feedback that had been coming my way by making my buddies laugh or by receiving support from the online forums, or even just the handshake I'd get from a stunned Lone Star manager, that I wasn't prepared for what to do when criticism or negativity was thrown my way. It wasn't something I was prepared for at all, and it took a little while just to get used to it. Giving in to the trolls and pulling that video is the one big regret I have hanging over my career.

The Pita Pit "challenge" was maybe the second.

CHAPTER 13

PITA PIT

*Challenge: Pita loaded with
70+ Pieces of Bacon*

{ TWO MINUTES }

Once I started eating competitively, I got it in my head that I was the king of eating. I was ready to take on any challenge that anybody threw at me, and that worked out about as well as you might expect.

My friends and I had gone out partying. Once we left the bars it was 3 a.m., and we were *starving*.

"We've got two options, guys," Adrian said. "Pizza or Pita Pit? That's all that's open." We looked over at the pizza place. It was overflowing with our wasted brethren, with the lone cashier looking like he was ready to jump out the window. Pita Pit it was. Blame it on the hunger, blame it on the drunkenness, but we started to wonder how big I could make my pita. When we got to the register, Gavin asked, "How big can you make the BLT?"

The guy shrugged. "I don't know. As big as you want? We sell extra orders of bacon for a dollar, so I guess you can make it as big as you're willing to pay for."

"Have you ever had someone make a huge BLT?" Adrian asked.

"Yeah, some dude once ordered one with like 21 orders of bacon..."

My buddies turned to me, "21 extra orders, which is 42 extra pieces of bacon on top of a normal BLT. All right, Pete, you got to beat this."

"You're buying?" I asked. He nodded. "All right then. Let's do this." So, we ordered what I think was 35 extra orders of bacon—or maybe it was 36 (it had been a hell of a night). My friend paid for it. It was like $44 for the one Pita. Once it came out though, I knew I would be the one paying for this decision in the end. It was just dripping puddles of grease. It was disgusting even to my drunk self. As the pita bread disintegrated in my hand under the full grease-saturation, I looked up at my friends. They hadn't even touched their food yet. They were just waiting for the horror show I was about to send into my intestinal tract. I looked back at the grease bomb. Then I looked back at them. Back at the bomb. Back at th—

"Go!" Gavin yelled.

No turning back now. "Okay," I said to myself, "I'm going to eat this. I'm going to do it." I finished it in about two (awful) minutes. Everyone around me was laughing and high-fiving, and I felt ready to die.

Not surprisingly, my "record" still stands there.

CHAPTER 14

I'M HUGE IN GERMANY

2007 to early 2008 was pretty much my show off year. It was the year where I discovered I had some talent, and every time I did a stunt, whether for a video or simply just for pictures or even just to do it, I got a big rise out of it. I was really good at something. It shocked just about everyone, but they also seemed to really enjoy my talent. All together, I got more praise and attention than I ever had in my life.

Then Igor, a director from Germany, contacted me asking if I was interested in coming to Germany to shoot some film of me eating my way around the country. "So, basically, it would just be me traveling around Germany eating mass portions of food?" I asked.

"Yes. We want a good personality. I am not really sure how your personality is, but that doesn't matter. We'll figure it out." He continued, "We just want you eating large portions of food. Maybe say a few lines if you think of something good."

At the time, I hadn't lost a contest yet. I was being referred to as "the Golden Child eating," and the rumor was that I couldn't be beaten. All that chatter caught this guy's eye. Igor worked with a production company for a network out in Germany called Pro Sieben for Kable and they were putting together a "Man vs. Food" meets "No Reservations" kind of show out there. The next thing I knew, I was on a flight out to Munich.

I was excited to be heading to Germany for the first time, but I had no idea what to expect. I figured even if the shoot was horrible and weird I would at least be getting a free trip to Europe. My plan was, "I'm going to extend this trip another week and travel around again afterwards," and with that in mind, I was up for whatever. Just as I had with my first eating contest, I walked into the room with no expectations.

"Peter, our plan is to go touring around Germany trying different kinds of foods," one of the producers began. "You won't always be eating large quantities; some times you will simply try unique foods of the area or popular things."

As they laid out what we would be doing, it all sounded good to me. We all shook hands then Igor said, "Let's get started," and started walking away.

I walked after him. "What are we doing?"

"Walking to the show bus," he said.

"Well, yeah, but where are we going?" I asked

"Oh, to the capital."

The first episode was just basically about showing my skills and showing how crazy I am. I was their little guinea pig, eating what they told me to as fast as I could. Igor was always looking for an angle that would add a little more "oomph" to the shoots too. If he could find a way to make it a little more controversial, he would. Which is how I ended up in front of the German government building in Berlin, shirtless, chugging a liter-and-a-half of water in five seconds for the camera.

"This is great, Pete," Igor said as he stepped past the crowd that had gathered around me. "It will be a hit, I'm sure."

"Glad to hear it," I replied. I had been keeping one eye on the capital guards since we'd arrived and I pulled my shirt off. Now it looked like one was making a move in our direction. "Hey, shirtless chugging on government property isn't something we could get arrested for, right?"

"I'm pretty sure it's not."

"Do you think that guy would agree?" I asked, pointing to the security guard.

"Maybe. Let's get back on the bus."

CHAPTER 15

TRAVEL STORIES

As it turned out, the show went really well. It wasn't long before Igor called me back. "We should do more." He and I teamed up and convinced the network to film some more episodes.

We started off in Europe. We did Austria, then we did Oktoberfest, then we toured Italy. Then we went over to Asia. We did Hong Kong, and we went to Thailand. Then we went to filming in the States a little bit. We filmed in Chicago. We filmed in Toronto. Then we went down to South America.

We filmed in Buenos Aires. We filmed in Brazil. Then we went back to Asia to film in Korea, South Korea. Then we did Kiev, and then we did Poland. After that, we did a tour across the States. We did New York City, Vegas, and LA. Then we did Beijing, Tokyo, Costa Rica, Marrakesh, Morocco, and Hawaii. We did a preview of the Sochi Olympics.

I could barely believe my good fortune.

Of course, some parts of the trip were a little rougher than others. Beginning with the 200th anniversary of Oktoberfest, a trip I can only remember because of the videos.

I had heard of Oktoberfest before, of course, but I didn't really know what to expect other than that it would be a party and a half. I was totally unprepared for the reality of Oktoberfest. There were 650,000 people in attendance. It's hard to imagine even now. There are massive tents that are built specifically for this event, and every tent can hold up to 15,000 people. The entire tent is lined with tables full of people drinking beer and listening to music, and it's an all-day event. Igor put a beer in my hand, and we started filming.

The focus of the show wasn't on me eating large portions of food. It was more of an exhibition. I went around just trying like different foods that they were serving within Oktoberfest. Obviously, this was for a German audience that knows about Oktoberfest. They relate to it when they see it. We tried a lot of things, mostly sweet stuff, and drank some beers. Then we went to a beer tent, ordered an entire chicken, demolished the chicken, and drank beers. From there, we found a hot dog stand. And I ate a meter-long hot dog. Then we had some beer.

I was drinking only casually, yet slowly but surely as the day wore on, I got more and more drunk. It took reviewing the day's footage to fill me in on the end of my day as I went around...surviving.

ASIA

Asia is a completely different world. It's so very different than anything back home—certainly different from anything I was used to. It's something that you have to experience once in your lifetime. There were lots of unique smells that I had never smelled before. It was a lot more busy, as a lot more people than I think I've ever seen in a single area flood the streets. I was stunned by how chaotic it felt. And I loved it.

I loved the diversity of the continent and the different flavors unique to each city. There was so much to try and, going around on these food tours, we had a lot of items that I never would have tried. We ate good items, tasty items, disgusting items, and we also had very, very unique and tasty items. Sometimes all in a single sitting.

The 1,000-Year-Old Egg and the Condom
{ HONG KONG }

"Of course it's not 1,000 years old, Pete," Igor told me. "That's just the name. It's only a few months old."

Essentially, I was about to eat a naturally cured egg. We were in Hong Kong and seated at a table at Bo Innovation, a molecular gastronomy restaurant known for its "X-treme Chinese." They've built an amazing reputation as one of Asia's top restaurants by playing around with different chemicals and gases to make their food do crazy things. Their take on the 1,000-year-old egg—or "Century Egg"—was, thankfully, way more advanced and gourmet than the traditional dish, which is made by basically coating an egg in salt, quicklime, and wood ash and letting it sit for a few weeks. As far as old, purple-black eggs go, this one wasn't so bad.

Then came the most terrible looking dessert I've ever had: the Sex on the Beach. The dish is made to look like a used condom—actually a cognac jelly mixture filled with a honey and condensed milk mixture—sitting on top of a pile of sand— actually powdered shitake mushroom. It looked so realistic I had to make the YouTube video age-restricted.

I glanced over at Igor, "Do I have to?"

He laughed at me. "I'm not going to pay you if you don't."

With that, I picked up what looked exactly like a used condom and ate it in one bite. My brain was really fighting me on that one. It just looked so much like the real thing and nothing like food. It's those sort of instances where I really struggle. Creamy stuff, smelly stuff, stuff that's still alive—those kinds of food are really hard for me to get down. Those are the times that my brain is telling me, "Hey, no, I don't want to eat this. It's not food. It's not food." But, never, ever has my brain fought me as hard as it did with the Sex on the Beach.

It Tastes...Chewy
{ HONG KONG }

On the very first night when we were in Hong Kong, we went to a hot pot restaurant, where they give you a bunch of raw ingredients then you cook it yourself in a pot kettle of simmering broth in front of you.

There were chicken feet, rooster testicles, ox testicles, bull testicles, chicken testicles, fish stomach, toad stomach, and a whole assortment of other unspeakable things.

I was definitely not the happiest of campers going in there. I was so tired of getting surprised with a different kind of animal penis. How many different ways can you say, "No, you made me eat *that*?" It was just terrible.

(Admittedly, the ox testicle wasn't that bad.)

I was amazed by the sheer amount of chewy foods put in front of me. When you go to an Asian restaurant and something is chewy, you know you've got something good apparently. This was a running gag. We would always just say, "It was chewy, so therefore, it must be good." It became one of our catchphrases. Our best catchphrase, however, would come when we were in Thailand.

"It was fantastic for my life."
{ THAILAND }

We flew to Bangkok, and I knew Igor had something up his sleeve. He loved dropping surprises on me in front of the camera.

"Igor," I asked him as we piled into the car, "where are we going?"

"To a restaurant, Pete."

As I was about to learn, Thailand has these restaurants and food stands that sell fried bugs. Grasshoppers, crickets, ants, you name it. I was about to eat a lot of it. One of the employees walked out and set a plate in front of me with 100 crickets piled on it.

I went straight into mind-over-matter mode and started eating them really fast, just stuffing my face, while Igor walked around with the camera to capture other people's reactions. He loved asking them questions like, "What did you think of this?" or saying, "This is stupid. Is he crazy?" He was always trying to get someone saying, "Oh my God, this guy is crazy."

He stopped at one guy, who was looking particularly "impressed" and asked him what he thought of my eating feat. His response became our biggest and most used phrase: "It was fantastic for my life and for every reason." We always laughed like crazy, saying this line every time something exciting happened. It was fantastic for my life.

Thankfully, not every meal in Thailand was meant to induce my gag reflex. One of the biggest highlights was eating a meal prepared by the king's chef. He took us to the market where he found all of the ingredients for our dinner. The meal itself was amazing, and the experience was so cool.

We went to the world's biggest restaurant in Thailand. It was so big that the servers had to all be on roller-skates to move quickly enough from end to end. I even did some Muay Thai boxing, thanks to Igor's perpetual attempts to get me to make a fool of myself.

He determined his favorite episode format was to try to find an activity for me that wasn't related to food at all. His ideal activities were ones that I was guaranteed to really suck at. Then, after I was good and embarrassed, we would do an eat-off of some sort so I could redeem myself. I tried (and failed at) Muay Thai boxing. I tried Kung Fu in Beijing; I tried sumo wrestling in Nara, Japan. And then we did some eating afterwards. While it's never the most fun to try something and look dumb as you struggle with it, I loved doing the different activities. It felt really good to connect with a country in that way—those things were often the unexpected highlights of my trips.

South Korea

There were few things Igor loved more than arranging for me to get my ass kicked. While we were in South Korea, which like all the Asian countries was unique and interesting, he set me up to do Tae Kwon Do with a local master. He *destroyed* me. At one point while we were filming, the master was trying to show me how he would hit me as part of one of the demonstrations—I had a block move that I was supposed to execute in order to deflect the blow. I must have missed, because he ended up hitting me, and I was totally winded out for like an hour because I guess he was good.

We went to the Korean barbecues. We learned how to make kimchi, but overall it was just a very busy country. We went over there before we went to Tokyo. Korea, South Korea, seemed like the most futuristic and most like, modern city that I'd ever been to at that point because there were lights everywhere in the city flashing this, flashing that. It just seemed very, very up-to-date compared to all the other places that we had been to so far.

You Don't Really Eat Spiders, Do You?
{ BEIJING, CHINA }

Some of the challenges we took on as a part of the world tour were, for lack of a kinder way to say, completely bullshit. They were tourist trap-style places that existed for no other reason than to help unsuspecting visitors spend their money on a "cultural" experience or a "local delicacy." These scenarios feel especially bullshit when it means that I have to eat spiders for essentially no reason.

We wandered over to a street in Beijing that is known for its different street food stalls, most of which just cook up a bunch of fried foods—and they'll fry anything if they think a dumb tourist will buy it. They cook up spiders, scorpions, snakes, all these random funny things that they would never actually eat and then wait for the tourists to come and pay a premium for the experience. At the end of the day, they're sitting in the back just laughing and thinking to themselves, "These people are idiots."

We didn't realize that until after I sat down for fried spiders. We were, after all, dumb tourists looking to film a "cultural experience." The king spiders were not tasty. They were just big and flavorless. They tasted like crispy nothings and left little bits of spider in my teeth, which, considering how much I dislike squirmy things, was pretty terrible.

I asked our fixer, "You guys don't really eat this, do you?"

He shook his head. "No. We don't eat this stuff," he motioned to Westerners all around us. "They think that we eat this stuff. We're just frying it up for them because they're willing to pay for it."

EUROPE

Schnitzel King
{ GERMANY }

Germany's Schnitzel King invited me out to compete against him. He had earned his title by winning a massive competition in Germany. He ate more schnitzel than anybody else, therefore he was the Schnitzel King. And, *man*, was he proud of it.

We met at a restaurant called Megaschnitzel, known for making schnitzel that weighs a kilo. He was very cocky as we sat down at the table, explaining to me all the ways he is the best eater and how proud he is of that fact. When our schnitzel, a long, thin piece of fried meat topped with some fries, showed up at our table, I casually took my first bite, smiled at the Schnitzel King, then I kicked his ass.

Then I asked for another schnitzel. After 15 minutes, I had beaten his record. I ordered another. And another. By the time our hour was up, I had not only broken the Schnitzel King's record, I had broken the World Record for most schnitzel eaten in a single hour: 4 kg (8.8 lbs.) The Schnitzel King did not handle his loss very well. He was unsuccessfully fighting back tears as we wrapped up the content.

Now, obviously, I would never want to make the Schnitzel King of Germany cry, but this guy had been so cocky beforehand that I didn't feel that bad about it. As far as I know, I am still the undisputed Schnitzel King of Germany.

"The Best in the World"
{ ITALY }

No matter where we went in Italy, every single restaurant or shop that we went to would tell us, "This is the best in the world."

"We have the best pasta in the world, the best linguine in the world, the best lasagna in the world, the best cheese in the world, the best salami in the world." And, of course, so much of what we were eating was incredible. Italian food is awesome. It's very, very filling, but it's delicious.

We headed south so I could compete in a pizza-eating contest against the best pizza eater in the south of Italy. This guy looked like he was, without question, involved with the mafia. He had won all of these contests throughout Naples and the South but, once it came time to face off over Neapolitan pizzas that were the size of an end table, I kicked his butt. I was sure not to rub my win in his face at all, given that I was convinced of his affiliation with *La Cosa Nostra*, and all things considered, he didn't seem to upset by the loss.

I didn't stick around too long after the contest though, just in case.

Spinning Doughnuts while Eating Doughnuts

{ NUREMBERG, GERMANY }

We came back to Germany for a two-week tour of the country in the dead of winter. It was easily minus 20 degrees Celsius everyday, which upped the crazy factor of some of our stunts.

We spent some time in Hamburg, where I got challenged with an 8-pound hamburger. I didn't think I would actually finish it for some reason. It just looked dense. But then I ended up destroying it.

Then we made our way to Nuremberg for a particularly harsh challenge that Igor had devised for me.

As we walked out of our Nuremberg hotel, Igor asked me, "Pete, do you know what the Nürburgring is?"

I shook my head.

"It's one of the most famous racing tracks and testing tracks for cars in the world."

"Oh, good," I said.

"Do you struggle with motion sickness?"

We drove down to the track and our contact there introduced

me to the professional racecar driver that would be taking me out for "a little drive." I was gung ho for the challenge, but it was a little disconcerting to watch the temperature get colder and colder and know without a shadow of a doubt that the track was going to be icy. It was even more disconcerting to get out to the car and see the ice on the track.

Igor clapped me on the back, handed me a box of doughnuts, and went back into the warm building. The plan was to do a bunch of laps in the car, while I sat in the passenger seat eating doughnuts. The challenge was to see how many donuts I could eat in one lap.

We took a couple laps around the track so I could get a sense of the timing, and then we started the challenge. I ended up eating 25 donuts in one lap. I probably could have done more, but because it was minus 20 degrees Celsius outside, the doughnuts had frozen solid by the time I got them into the car. Chomping down on a frozen pastry wasn't too much fun, and it made eating an entire bag of them a lot harder than what it was supposed to be.

When we pulled the car back in, Igor came out, "Pete, well done! How are you feeling?"

"Good," I said. "I feel good."

"Excellent!" He said, "There is a pizza challenge happening in the city today. I think we should film there if you're up for it."

That's how I ended up competing in a ten-pound pizza

challenge an hour after eating 25 donuts in a racecar. It was an awfully weird, painful day. After the pizza challenge, I could start to feel the impact of all those carbs and sugars slogging through my body. Shutdown was imminent. Stacking challenges of any kind is pretty rough, but the one-two punch of doughnuts and pizza KO'd me. We climbed back into the car to head back to the hotel, and it was an awfully good thing that I wasn't driving. I passed out in the back of the car within minutes.

SOUTH AMERICA

Lost. Again.
{ BUENOS AIRES }

I don't know that I've ever been lost as much as I was lost in Buenos Aires. We were given a guide, a lovely older woman named Carol, whose job was to take us around town and make sure we got where we were going easily and on time.

Whenever we filmed in another country, we arranged to have a fixer, someone who spoke the language and knew the area well enough to keep our lives easy—and make sure that we have all the permissions we need to film in every location we plan to film in.

Carol came to us with what we thought would be a lot of useful experience. She said she worked with big production companies before and television hosts like Andrew Zimmern and Anthony Bourdain, which sounded perfect. Then she got behind the wheel, and we were pretty sure she was full of shit.

We always knew when something had gone awry when Carol would call back to us, "Okay, Plan B...Okay, Plan D...Okay, Plan E." The same thing would happen when we'd learn at the last minute that we couldn't film where we originally planned. Then we'd pile back in the van and head off in a new direction that we'd eventually have to retrace our steps back from.

It took us ten times longer to get to every location than it would have if we had just fired up the GPS, but she refused to use one. She truly thought she knew where she was going. She just never did.

"Okay, now we're going to go to the San Telmo neighborhood," as she veered the van to the right (when we all knew we needed to go left). We sat back and waited for the van to turn around as Carol called out, "Plan Z, okay!"

Despite being lost for half the time, Buenos Aires was really cool and a great place to eat. I actually tackled an ostrich leg—an *entire* ostrich leg. That thing was massive. I never thought I would be served meat that size, or that it would even exist. It was absolutely gigantic.

The ostrich leg had the "quantity" angle covered, while the beef was easily the highest quality I've ever had. Their cows are just different. You can get a steak that is just so well marbled that you could cut it with a spoon, and they're not even

aged! Those phenomenal steaks were easily the highlight...
even if I had to dress up like a flashy cowboy to get them.

Argentinian cowboys, or gauchos, are probably some of the
fanciest looking cattle wranglers out there. They can do these
insane tricks on horseback, which cancels out the fact that
they're wearing a little hat, a scarf, and puffy pants tucked into
their tall, skinny boots. No one is going to give those guys a
hard time because they're so good at what they do. Unfortunately, the same does not apply for the big, white Canadian guy
who can barely climb into a saddle. I looked ridiculous, but I
still had a good time. It wasn't until I got home to Toronto and
realized that all my friends had managed to get their hands
on the pictures of me in a gaucho costume that I was able to
feel some full-force embarrassment.

Where's the Croc?
{ BRAZIL }

Ordinarily, our filming was never particularly dependent on
the weather outside. There was always some improvisation
at food stands and vendors, but, for the most part, we were
going into restaurants and cafes, ordering up their menu and
then I'd take down all the food. If it was raining outside, no
big deal. Unfortunately, this was not the case in Rio de Janeiro.

I knew it was going to be rough as we ascended the steps of the
famous Jesus statue, Christ the Redeemer, to film the classic
"hey, we're in Brazil" shot for our footage. Even at the base of

the statue, you couldn't see the big Jesus through the clouds and the rain. The bad weather continued for most of our stay, which also made it difficult to get our shots with the roadside stands and open-air café's we had planned to hit. We shifted into full-improvise mode, with Igor saying things like, "Hey, go eat all the cheese balls in that case."

Our guide was of no help as we tried to build backup plans. He didn't give a fuck. 90% of the time he was on the phone, but I was sure he was only actually talking to someone 20% of that time. He knew he didn't do enough research to set us up, so he was constantly on the phone so we couldn't yell at him. He wasn't calling anyone to rectify the situation. He just knew we were mad at him.

One instance was particularly egregious. We wanted to get some shots in a rainforest or jungle—we were, after all, in Brazil.

"We want to shoot some footage in a jungle."

"Oh yeah, yeah, yeah. There's a great jungle in the city."

We thought that was a little weird but figured it must be a preserve or a national park, so we went along.

We get up to this "jungle" that looked exactly like Central Park.

I'm on a huge paved walkway, and I crouch down into some leafy bushes to look like I'm in the jungle. It made no sense. We were clearly not in a jungle.

He also told us he would set us up with some of the best *futbol* players in Brazil to show me some moves and run me up and down the field. As we pulled up to the field, I didn't see any pros. I just saw a group of 12-year-olds.

"These are the pros, huh?" I asked our guide. He was on the phone.

We filmed in Brazil for four or five days and then I stayed for an extra two weeks on my own. This was something I did more and more as our shooting locations got more exotic. My thinking was, "Hell, I'm already here. Might as well make the most of it. It's going to be fun to see more things."

I went out to a place called the Pantanal, which is a mix of flatlands and jungle in the western part of Brazil, close to the border of Argentina. I spent 5 days with two guides in tents in the middle of nowhere with zero communication. We traveled all over as they showed me everything.

One afternoon, we were sitting near the water when one of the guides asked me, "Have you ever tried crocodile?"

I thought for a second, taking inventory of the range of land and sea creatures I had tried over the course of my travels and realized that crocs were not on the list. I was actually kind of surprised. "No," I said, "I haven't."

"Great," they said. "We're going to have some Cayman crocodile tonight."

"Okay, that's cool," I replied almost automatically. Then the gears in my head started turning. *How are we going to get the crocodile?*

I followed them down to the water, wondering what the hell I was about to see. What happened next didn't disappoint. With nothing but a rope snare, these guys waded into the water up to their knees.

Everything I'd ever seen on the Discovery Channel rushed back to me—all the biting fish, the carnivorous insects, the massive, *massive* snakes, and how much they loved the exposed skin of over-daring humans. I realized I was expecting to see the water frothing around them or see one of them go under suddenly as he got dragged away by something terrifying. I didn't look away though because I knew this was going to be awesome.

Sure enough, they hunted down a crocodile with a rope and their bare hands. One guide grabbed the croc with the snare and proceeded to reach into the water to hold on to its thrashing body. The other guide took a quick step forward and then hit it with his fist. They didn't have any weapons.

They dragged the Cayman to the shore and, using a machete, cut off the tail. Then they walked over to me, smiling and holding up the tail. "Dinner."

I was stunned. I had no words as I turned and followed them back to the tent.

Once I got ahold of myself, I was able to muster, "That was insane."

They both laughed as they built up the fire to cook the tail. "Call it the tour highlight. You'll like the Cayman too. It's very good."

"Can I ask you guys something though?" I responded. "Why didn't you use the machete when you caught him? It probably would have been easier."

"Easier, yes," replied one of the guides. "But where's the fun? Now you will tell all your friends."

He had me there. With that, I stood up and realized I had left my camera sitting on the sand where I had watched them catch the croc. I retraced my steps back to the water, grabbed my camera, and turned to take a picture of the croc we had caught.

It was gone.

Holy shit. I don't want to say I sprinted back to our tents, but saying it any other (braver) way would be a complete lie. "Guys," I said as I tried to slow my obvious fleeing to a casual stroll, "the Cayman is gone. Are you sure it was dead?"

"Not really. It was dead or it was unconscious. It was the same for our purposes," one of the guides said, motioning to the tail cooking on the fire.

"So, it's possible that it's awake, angry, and trolling around?" I asked.

"I'm guessing something ate it."

"Right," I said, "of course." I couldn't decide which thought was scarier: the tailless crocodile with a vengeance or the anaconda that was big enough to eat him. For the rest of the night, I jumped at the slightest sound of movement while the guys who can catch crocodiles with their hands laughed their asses off.

CHAPTER 16

YOUTUBE STAR

I had been filming episodes with German television for close to two years before I started blowing up on YouTube. What really pushed me over the edge and got me popular was the fact that I started listening to the formula that you have to do on YouTube, which is trying to be consistent and put content on a weekly basis. Over the years, I started to pick up the quantity, which I'm sure helped me.

But, really, it's all about quality, listening to what fans want to see and then giving it to them. I was always pretty good at that part because I really enjoyed it. It's what really pushed me personally. Obviously, if you have viral videos, that helps out all the time. I've had a few here and there that helped me out. At the end of the day, it's about being consistent on there.

That's why you see those celebrities that can be on YouTube, they'll have the top sellers, top box hit movies, but they'll do a YouTube channel. They won't have that many followers overall because it's a totally different game. The "Furious Pete World Tour," as we called it, helped me make huge strides in learning these things that have since proved so crucial to my professional life.

Then there were the more personal lessons that came from traveling to places that were so different from my own country and trying new things that were so far outside my comfort zone. It did amazing things for my confidence and for my mentality at large.

Even the failed challenges and bad-tasting foods yielded a positive outcome; they pushed me to keep going—to *do* whatever it was I was there to do—even when I didn't want to. It's amazing how effective it is to have a camera in your face. There were many times (especially when I was sitting in front of something chewy) when I caught myself thinking, "There's no chance of me finishing this. But I'm here right now, so I might as well try. We have cameras rolling. I might as well just at least try it."

My life requires an interesting level of mind over matter. It comes into play all the time. As I've learned, you can tell yourself, "Just try. You might fail, but just try it," or you tell yourself, "Yes, you can do this because you've done things like these before."

Whether I was eating strange foods or willingly throwing myself onto a Thai boxing mat, these challenges pushed me mentally in a way that was very positive. It's something that I would recommend to anyone: try the strange food and try the new activity. If you get nervous, tell yourself to keep going and just stay calm. Stay with yourself, close your eyes, and push through whatever is front of you.

Beforehand, I just get nervous, and I'm just like, "I can't do this. I can't do this." That's what I tell myself most of the time when I catch myself feeling nervous and thinking *I can't do this.* And then once I just get started, the script changes to *Okay, let's do this.*

Then I go for it.

CHAPTER 17

WORLD RECORDS

Growing up I always loved the Guinness Book of World Records. I probably had 10 of the books in my house, and I'd flip through them all the time, gawking at the guy with the world's longest fingernails, the shortest woman in the world standing next to the world's tallest man, and the guy wearing the suit of bees—more bees than anyone in the world. My friends and I would speculate which records we might be able to break. We might have even attempted one or two when we were little. I never dreamed I'd have my picture in the book one day.

Once I was eating competitively and breaking records, I got it in my head that I should go after a Guinness record. For most records, it still requires a pretty formal process. You've got to be in an approved setting with an official on hand to make sure there's no funny business. Some, however, can be done more informally by recording a video and posting it online. I started hunting these opportunities down and found one that sounded really unpleasant but totally doable: eat a whole, raw onion faster than anyone in the world.

There were several specifications in place. The onion had to be a white cooking onion—it couldn't be a sweet onion or even a red onion. It had to be at least 210 grams after peeling the skin off. It had to be totally raw. I could drink water but nothing else. Time started when I picked up the onion, and it didn't stop until my mouth was clear. The time to beat was 45 seconds, a record that had stood for the last 5-6 years.

I used two different cameras set at two different angles. (I had finally upgraded to a real video camera by this time.) I hit the record buttons and got started. First, I weighed out the onion on camera, then I set it back down and cued up my timer. Then I picked up the onion and tore into it. I finished the onion, opened my mouth to the cameras to show that it was empty, and checked my timer. *Dammit.* I got 49 seconds. So close! Fortunately, I bought a backup onion.

I took a couple minutes to psych myself back up and launched into my second attempt. This time I did it in 43.53 seconds. My first Guinness Record!

I sent in my video and a few weeks later the Guinness Book of World Records made it official and sent me a certificate. I thought it was the coolest thing and was practically ecstatic as I opened up the envelope. It was framed and on my wall almost immediately. It was the best thing ever...until I was asked again and again to perform my record-breaking feat again. Every TV show I went on wanted me to break this record again.

I don't know what it is. You can cook up some onion or eat it in a salad and you're totally fine. But if you eat a whole onion, especially a cooking onion, it stays in your system for three days. You sweat onion, you smell like an onion, and you taste onion on everything. It is the worst experience ever. Now I was eating multiple onions a day as I made appearances on different shows.

Once I had to stare down a third onion in a single day, I declared myself done. I vowed to never do it again. You can't taste anything, you smell terrible, and nobody wants to be around you. Unless someone is willing to pay me a stupid amount of money, I will not do it. And if someone else beats my record, they can have it.

CHAPTER 18

DALE BOONE

I had been on such a winning streak that I suppose it was just a matter of time before people started trash talking me and trying to get into my head before competitions. The more I started winning, the more confident I got, and the more people would try to get in my head.

Dale Boone, another competitive eater, was one of those guys. Dale is one of those guys who talks trash to every single individual out there. He thinks that it gives him an edge going into the actual competition, and he loves it. He loves to compete against everyone and likes to trash talk against everyone. To Dale, it's all part of the game.

He had been around for a long time—probably ten years—before I even started doing eating challenges. But coming into this competition, we had already squared off against one another ten times—and I won every single one of them.

It was the third annual Z Burger eat-off in Washington, D.C. I had won the previous two competitions and was looking to get my first career three-peat. This event always has a big media presence too. There are always 10 different television stations, and they're all recording. The fan presence is huge too. In other words, I was either going to emerge from this competition as a three-time champ, or I'd be the overthrown favorite. Between that and Dale's trash talking, I was feeling the pressure.

I'm a speed eater. I'm a power eater, and when it comes to competition "strategy," I just jump right in and get a head start. So, I'll start a contest, and I'll go up two on top of everyone else as quickly as possible. This contest was no different. I went up two burgers ahead of everyone else right away.

Dale Boone was in the second place position, but, with just a minute left to go, I was a full three burgers ahead of him. I figured I had the competition locked up and could start coasting. Then, with seconds left to go, I took a look at the totals and realized Dale and I were tied. It happened all of the sudden, and now I didn't have time to eat one more burger to take the win. The clock hit zero and both of us had 14 and a half burgers as our final total. I couldn't believe it. I looked over at Dale wondering, "Whoa, how did that happen? I was good. I had it in the bag."

The event organizers weren't prepared for a tiebreaker scenario and were gathered together to figure out how to proceed. It didn't seem like there could be any way to resolve the tie except for another contest. The organizers agreed. They walked over and told me, "All right, we're going to do an eat-off really soon. Don't go anywhere."

And so we step back. I walked up to my girlfriend, Melissa, and asked her, "How in the world did he catch up to me?"

"Honestly," she replied, "I have no idea. He wasn't even close until the very, very end."

Everyone was standing around talking. The organizers were trying to figure out how to hold this tiebreaker. We were trying to figure *why* I was going to have to compete in a tiebreaker in the first place.

Then Joe, one of my fellow competitive eaters, tapped me and pointed toward Dale's table. "Look at his cups. Why are they so dark?"

Meat tends to be kind of difficult at times just because there is nothing that you can do to meat to make it go down in a faster way. You have to chew it and eat it. With a lot of bread products, things like that, you can soften it up with water, make it softer and then stuff down the meat. As we all know from watching the Nathan's Hot Dog Eating Challenge, you can take a hot dog and a bun and dip that entire bun in a cup of water (as gross as that sounds) and put it in your mouth and swallow it without chewing at all. Dale was probably dipping his burgers into his cups, but that wasn't a big deal as far as the rules were concerned.

"It's probably Crystal Light," I said. "A lot of times competitive eaters will either drink water or they'll sometimes put Crystal Light inside to just flavor their water so that it can kill the taste of the food. It's legal."

"Even so, they look weird. Look at his cups."

We stepped back and looked closer at Dale's setup. He had five or six plastic cups sitting on his table, and the light was hitting them just enough that we could see the color of the drink inside. These cups were big—at least 32 ounces—and two of them were glowing a red color, the color of Crystal Light. The rest of them though, the *majority* of them, were really dark.

I looked at my friends, "You're right, dude. That's not right. Something is definitely off." As my friends started talking about what the reason behind the color change could be, I stood silently for a second. I knew what it was. The answer moved through my head right away. "I know exactly why they're so dark." Dale had a suspicious, if not notorious, reputation in competitive eating circles. He loved to win, and he wasn't afraid of trying to gain advantages where he could.

Without a word, I started walking toward Dale's side, right toward his cups. Dale called out, "What are you doing? Why are you going up to my cups? What do you think you're doing?"

Without breaking my stride, I looked over at him. "I need to see something."

He started moving toward me as I got to his table. "No, no, no you don't. Stop trying to be a sore loser."

"I'm not trying to be a sore loser," I said, "I just want to see something." And then I put my hands into the cups.

Dale grabbed my arms immediately, trying to pull my hands out of the cups right away, and all of a sudden, all the media was right on us. Ten different cameras were on top of us as we struggled over these cups of reddish purple liquid. I yank my hands out of the two cups with two fistfuls of big chunks of burger. I looked at Dale as I dropped them on the table. Then I moved down his line of cups, pulling food out of every single one of them. I shoved all the food on the table to show everyone exactly what just happened.

"You're such a sore loser, Pete," Dale continued. I couldn't believe he was still trying to call me out when I had just exposed his cheating. It was funny for a quick second but then it got heated.

Dale kept chirping, and, while I didn't really care, my girlfriend had had enough of him. She went up into his face and started yelling at him. It was amazing. Ordinarily she's very restrained, yet here she was using all the power she had inside her not to punch him in the mouth.

In the middle of this ridiculous fray, the lead organizer inserted himself. "Hey guys, it's time for the eat-off. We're going to do a one minu—"

"He cheated," I interrupted, pointing to the pile of Crystal Light-soaked meat on Dale's table. "We don't need to have a tie-breaking eat-off because there wasn't an actual tie."

The organizer glanced toward the scene of the crime and then turned back to us. "Okay, so like I said, it's going to be a one-minute eat-off. Most burgers wins. Head back to your tables, and we'll get started."

I didn't understand why they didn't just disqualify Dale, but they didn't. We held an eat-off instead, and I still crushed him. I ate three burgers to his one, and, for the first time in probably ever, Dale Boone walked away in absolute silence.

CHAPTER 19

CLINTON STATION DINER

Challenge: Zeus Burger
{ DQ }

In almost every eating challenge I've ever done, there has come a moment when I look at the plate of food in front of me and think to myself, "This was a bad idea. Why am I doing this?" Then there are challenges where I can look at my plate and immediately know, "Ah, damn, I got screwed. There's no way I'm going to finish this." I had one of those the first year I was competing.

I had done a few contests already, and I destroyed everyone. I mean *destroyed*. Nobody came close to me in every single one. And I had this mindset that said, "I can kill everything. I can beat everything. There's nothing that can stand in my way."

So when I heard about the Zeus Burger challenge at the Clinton Station Diner, a 12 pound burger and a $500 prize for finishing it, I figured I'd waltz in and destroy their records too. I was in New York for a contest and had a few extra days on the itinerary, so I decided to make the hour-long drive to check it out.

I walked in super-confidently and ordered it up along with all this other stuff. The second it came out, though, I knew they were trying to screw me. This burger was *way* more than 12 pounds; it looked like it weighed more like 19 pounds. I looked over at my friend Joel, who was shaking his head. Fortunately, he had brought a scale with him. We put the whole thing on the scale and to no surprise the thing weighed between 18 and 19 pounds.

We were like, "What the hell? You guys screwed us."

The managers didn't even look surprised. They just shrugged and said, "Oh, well, that's the challenge. If you don't do it, you'll have to pay for it." I couldn't believe it.

My choices then were 1) walk out right then and there, pay for the burger, get in the car, and drive back to the city, or 2) give it a shot and see how far I could get. So, I ended up trying it.

The challenge was, in a word, undoable. The patty—if you can call it that—basically was more of a meat loaf instead of a burger. It was so much meat. And then they make their own buns, and by buns I mean it was topped with a foot-wide bagel. It was a super, super dense bun. If the extra weight was coming from anywhere, it was that bun. I shook my head and looked at my buddies a final time before picking up my knife and fork.

I started eating, and I actually ended up finishing close to 70 percent of it—which basically means that if it were made the right way, I would have beaten the challenge just as I knew I could. Instead, it was the first notable live challenge I failed as a newly minted pro.

CHAPTER 20

DUMPLING CONTEST

Whether you're a competitor or the place hosting the competition, cheating to win an eating challenge seems so pointless to me. Dale Boone wasn't the only guy willing to pull strings to make a win happen, just as the Clinton Station Diner wasn't the first to orchestrate a loss. As in the case of the New York dumpling eating contest, there are others who are perfectly willing to set up a guaranteed loss for a specific person.

In 2009, I entered a dumpling-eating contest in New York City. The reigning champion was a guy named Joe Menchetti. He had won the contest for four years in a row prior to this, and his title mattered to him. He knew all the people that were running the competition, which is always helpful when you need to secure a win, especially when you're facing a guy that you've consistently lost to the way Joe was about to face me. Prior to this contest I had beat him in every single challenge that we competed against each other in. I just beat him in everything. He never even came close. So, I guess he felt like his title was really on the line and decided he was willing to do anything he could to beat me.

This contest was a two-minute eating contest. We had 120 seconds to eat as many dumplings as humanly possible. However, there were 40 competitors, and, as a result, they had to divide it into four rounds. So, there would be 10 people that went first. They would take their totals, and then the next round would go and the next round and then the final round would go. This was Joe's opportunity. He talked the organizers into putting me into the first round, and then he put himself into the last round.

Going in the first round meant that I didn't have a set number goal; I was simply up against the clock. I did the best I could in two minutes. Joe, on the other hand, had this number that he was striving for—my number—which is a much different mindset. It pushes you in a certain way.

I set a number of 52 in two minutes and was winning by a lot going into the fourth round. Then Joe stepped up, and he was flying through the dumplings. He was, after all, a man with a number to hit. And he did. With just a second or two to go, Joe had 52 dumplings down. And then, somehow, he managed another dumpling at the very end. Don't even ask me how. Everyone tells me that he snorted the 53rd one through his nose at the very end. He beat me by one as a result.

That loss hurt. It really sucked. There had never been any animosity between us for the most part. I didn't have any hate towards the guy. I still don't. I've since competed with him, and we've always had friendly conversation. It was rough at first though. Going into that day, everyone thought I was unbeatable, unstoppable. I had thought that too, to be honest. For two years, no one touched me, and this loss stung a little extra because I felt like it could have ended very differently.

CHAPTER 21

WING BOWL

Wing Bowl. Good old Wing Bowl.

Wing Bowl is a contest that happens every single year in the beginning of February, right around the Super Bowl. Competitive eaters come into Philadelphia from all over for this competition, and it's so much more than an eating competition. For one thing, it starts at 8:00 a.m. Tailgating starts at 4:00 a.m. The crowd numbers around 20,000 people. There are people drinking. There are porn stars there. And then, in the middle of all the craziness, there's a 30-minute wing-eating contest. It consists of two 14-minute rounds and then a 2-minute final round, and the competitor field is *massive*.

The first round knocks out a ton of people. Those who make it to the second round are then gathered together for the second 14-minute round. Then they take the top five for the last two minutes. This was a contest I really wanted to win. I had to qualify to get into it, and it came with a $20,000 prize for the winner.

The challenge I completed to earn my place at Wing Bowl was a rough one. It had to be a radio stunt, as in I had to come in to do an eating stunt on the radio, and the theme of my challenge came from a line in *Cool Hand Luke*: "No man can eat 50 eggs." My challenge was to prove Clint Eastwood wrong.

So, I ate 50 hard-boiled eggs in 10 minutes. At 6:00 a.m. It was awful, but I won my spot.

Once I had qualified, the warnings started rolling in. "Don't do Wing Bowl," one of my friends told me, "The contest is rigged."

"What do you mean 'rigged'?" I asked.

"They set it up so the local always wins."

I didn't really take the warning seriously. Instead, I simply said, "No, no. I'm good enough. I'm going to crush everyone." Despite my loss in the dumpling contest, I still was in an unstoppable mind set.

Once again, my friends and I loaded up the car and started driving. This competition/party was so big and well known that I had no trouble putting together a bunch of friends for this contest. It was a good thing too because I had to ride on a parade float—and who doesn't want a bunch of witnesses for that?

It's one of the funnier parts of Wing Bowl—the parade of competitors on their homemade floats making their way around the stadium before the contest starts. My float was absolute garbage. Since we were driving down from Canada, we didn't have space (and weren't willing to tow) a homemade float. So, I had somebody else make one for me and gave them little instruction; instead, my "instructions" were the two-word phrase that has never, ever lead to regret: "Surprise me." The quality of the final product should come as no surprise. I think the general theme was "Canada," and the centerpiece was supposed to be a moose. But instead of a moose, they had just stuck one of those small plastic reindeer lawn ornaments in the middle and put a droop pair of antlers on it. And then they added an axe and a hockey stick because I suppose it added to the overall Canadian-ness. It was a very, very sad, sad float.

After the early tailgating and busted parade, it was competition time. We did the first round, and I was on a roll: 178 wings in 14 minutes. But when the final totals rolled around, I looked up at the scoreboard, and my mouth fell open. There, next to my name, was the number 138. They had knocked 40 wings off my total.

For a minute, my mind was factoring possible causes. "Maybe they hit the wrong button?" "Maybe they crossed my score with someone else?" But deep down, I knew immediately what was up. Finally, my brain caught up. "Oh, no, it *is* rigged. Fuck."

I was really pissed off. Then in the next round, another 14-minute round, I simply just lost motivation to compete. I was in second place when I started the second round—thanks to them lowering my totals. I finished third in the second round, which knocked me into fourth place going into the final round. And then I just didn't care because I knew they just wouldn't let me win. I didn't try at all.

Sure enough a local won. It didn't come as a surprise. I was told I would lose, and lo and behold, I did. Needless to say, I haven't been back to Wing Bowl since.

CHAPTER 22

KOBAYASHI

"Kobayashi left Major League Eating."

I looked over at Melissa, who was scrolling through an article on her phone. "Really?"

"Yep, she said, "Says it right here."

Takeru Kobayashi, arguably one of the most famous competitive eaters ever and most known for his streak of demolishing performances at the Nathan's Hot Dog Challenge in Coney Island, was like my white whale. He was the guy I most wanted to compete against, but we were never able to go head-to-head.

For years, Kobayashi was part of Major League Eating, a competitive eating league. I, on the other hand, was essentially a free agent (though I had been a member of a different league when I first started competing), so I couldn't enter into the contests he was competing in. I never got an opportunity to face off against the best. Now Kobayashi had left MLE because he wanted more freedom, which meant I could finally have a run against him.

I looked back over at Melissa. "That is *awesome* news."

Despite the string of losses at Wing Bowl, Clinton Station Diner, and the dumpling-eating contest, my confidence was riding high. I was boosted by a recent wave of competition victories and felt like I was back to my usual winning streak. I had been riding high for so long, winning contest after contest, that I thought I was invincible. I was ready to take on the king.

The showdown finally happened at a huge event in Ontario at a place called Pie. It was a pizza-eating contest to see who could eat the most in 12 minutes. Despite the fact that it was dumping rain, more than 200 people had shown up to watch us compete.

The pizzas were thin-crust (thank god) and topped with basil, tomato, and mozzarella. Simple enough. The contest started, and Kobayashi and I were off to the races. For seven minutes, I went slice for slice with him. The pizzas were cut into four big slices, which made for easy folding and chomping, and I felt like I was on a roll. Then all of a sudden, I started to feel like I hit a brick wall. I looked over at Kobayashi, and he hadn't even slowed down. He kept going at the exact same pace—no slowdown, no struggle. He didn't even look tired.

Shit. I thought. *I don't even stand a chance anymore.*

At the end of the contest, he had eaten 40 slices—10 full pizzas—and I came in with only 29 slices. He had smoked me, but I was really happy that I got to compete against him.

The most telling thing for me was the way the contest, and the fact that I hit the wall, showed me the difference in how I competed and the way that Kobayashi did. I never trained capacity. I had always just approached it in a natural way. "I'll just try this, and if I'm good at it, great. If not, whatever." Kobayashi's ability was a clear indicator of what is possible when someone takes what he does so seriously and trains his body for years to get good at it. It was just so impressive.

After the contest, I went up to congratulate him. I shook his hand. "It was such an honor to compete against you." He replied, telling me that he had worried about me prior to the contest. He was nervous that I would come out of nowhere and kick his ass. He pushed very hard to make sure that he would win. He wanted to bury me. And he did.

He has consistently kicked my ass every time we've competed against one another...but I have taken three of his Guinness World Records.

CHAPTER 23

COMPETITIVE EATING CAN BE DANGEROUS

Without question, my least favorite food to eat competitively is hot dogs. I hate them. Worse, I hate the feeling of so many hot dogs in my body. Hot dogs and their insane sodium content make me feel terrible. Still, in terms of pure physical pain, there is nothing worse than ghost peppers.

Actually, that's not true. There's nothing worse than eating ghost peppers *with a gaping hole inside your mouth.*

I had entered a ghost pepper burrito-eating contest, but in the days leading up to the challenge, developed a mucous cell inside my mouth. I basically had a water bubble inside my lip. It was so big it looked like my entire lip was swollen. There was nothing I could do about it though. If I popped the little bubble, it would just fill up with fluid all over again.

I went to the doctor to get it looked at, and he told me the only way to get rid of it was surgery. "It's a quick minimally invasive procedure. We have you in and out before the end of the afternoon."

So I said, "Let's do it," not at all thinking about the fact that I was going to have to eat a bunch of extraordinarily spicy food just a few days later.

I had surgery to get the mucous cell removed from the lip and came home with my mouth bandaged up and a pocketful of antibiotics. It was then, as I was changing the dressing on the gaping hole in my lip that I remembered the upcoming contest.

"Ah, shit. That's going to hurt, but it's too late to back out now," I thought. "I have to do it." The news got worse as I reread the competition guidelines. I would have to compete to qualify for the final round, and then compete in the finals a few hours later. Each round consisted of a one-pound burrito chock full of ghost peppers. "One pound, that's not so bad," I thought. "I can take it down fast and be done with it."

There have been plenty of moments when I've sat down for a contest and immediately had second thoughts about what I was about to do, but none of those moments were as immediate and certain as when that first ghost pepper burrito was put in front of me. I could see the big pieces of chili bulging through the tortilla. The damn thing even hurt to *smell*. "Just avoid your lip," I thought. Then the *go* sounded, and I bit into pure, unadulterated, white-hot, pain.

I destroyed the burrito as fast as humanly possible, winning the qualifying round with ease, but my mouth, or more specifically the *open wound* in my mouth, felt like it was about to actually catch fire. The pain managed to be dull and searing at the same time—like a red hot poker dipped in slow moving flesh-eating acid—as it radiating throughout my entire skull, basically making it impossible to do anything but stare straight at the ground, hoping for the cooling relief of sweet, sweet death.

"Way to go, Pete! One more set of ghost peppers and you're walking away with the win!" my buddy Nick said.

I wondered whether lip-ectomies were a thing as a single tear worked its way down my face.

"Dude," Nick said, "are you okay?"

"I don't know, man," I said while trying to hold my lip as far away from my teeth as I could. I flipped my lip out to show him the inside of it. "How does it look?"

"You ate ghost peppers with a fucking *hole* in your mouth! What the hell is the matter with you?" he said, jumping back.

"I don't think I can eat the next one."

"You *think*?"

"I'll make it a game time decision."

I really didn't want to, but I ended up being in so much pain that I had to withdraw from the finals. By that time, my surgery site had become really red, and I was worried another ghost pepper burrito would make it worse (and I try to avoid scenarios that might make me cry in public). It was just so painful, and it continued to hurt for hours afterwards. Ghost-pepper-in-the-wound pain sticks with you too. My mouth still recoils in spice-based PTSD when I see those demon chilies.

Competitive eating isn't glamorous. That's for sure.

Whether they're spicy, sloppy, or soaked in maple syrup, the challenges I take on aren't for the faint of heart, and the characters that you see coming to these contests are just desperate to win. They'll do whatever it takes to win. They'll try and hide food; they will choke, gag, and vomit; they will get really messy, with water soaked bits of food flying into their hair and sticking to their skin and clothes; they'll even sacrifice their health. People will do anything just to come in first place.

A lot of those people have nothing else going on in their lives except for eating and trying to do these contests. They don't exercise, and they don't eat particularly healthy even on their off days. And because of that, they are significantly, *significantly* overweight. It's a tough crowd to be a part of when you actually *do* care about your health the way that I do.

Little by little, I've started to phase myself out of eating competitively. I do hardly any competitions now. But it took me a little while to get to that point, and it took a scary incident to drive it home.

The first incident came when I was on UK television. I had set the Guinness World Record for eating a 12-inch pizza a few months beforehand. And ITV, the big, big, *big* network in the UK, invited me to come up to appear on their show, "Let's Do Lunch." They arranged a pizza-eating contest between the host and me. It was all in good fun, but the pizza came in extremely undercooked. As I tried to compete, one of the slices got lodged in my throat. I was choking for the first time in my career. I couldn't breathe at all.

Everyone around me thought I was puking and stepped away from me. Somehow I managed to dislodge the pizza and get it out of me. "No, I was really choking," I told them afterward. It wasn't the first time a piece of food had got caught in my throat. It had happened several times before. I had been able to just eat more and push it down, so it was never really a negative outcome. This time, though, was my first big scare. It spooked me and added a new level of cautiousness to the way I approach my competitive eating. It's a fun thing for me to do, but I'm not about to let it kill me.

CHAPTER 24

THE DOCUMENTARY

There's little glamour in competitive eating. Between the piles of food, the mess you make when you tear through them at top speed, and the digestive carnage that happens after the fact, there aren't a whole lot of people out there who admire what I do. They're impressed, sure, but it isn't a line of work many would choose for themselves. Then there are those who criticize it. Competitive eating takes a lot of flack for food waste, and, while the contests are entertaining events, they don't exactly give back to the community. "Competitive eating has no soul" is an accusation I've heard more than once, which is pretty harsh.

My parents were on the supportive end of the spectrum, fortunately, but they didn't quite know what to make of my eating. They thought it was stupid, obviously, but they also saw I was making some money and getting to travel for free. So, they never gave me a hard time for doing it, but they didn't really see the point either. They hadn't even watched my YouTube videos, let alone attended a live event.

That changed when I went down to Baltimore to compete in back-to-back eating contests: a wing contest and a corned beef contest. My father had joined me on the trip, which was awesome. It was one of the first times my parents actually came to see what my competitive eating thing was all about.

It was really fun to see his reaction. He actually seemed to be enjoying himself! Prior to that day, my dad didn't really understand what I was doing with competitive eating. Now that he was in the moment, saw how close it was, how aggressive people get, and how much tension is in the room, he was getting really into it.

He was nervous before the finals. "I've got butterflies in my stomach over this. You gotta do this, Pete. You gotta eat fast." Then he was *so* excited when I won. He had tapped into the adrenaline factor and was now fully in my corner. He must have gone home and told my mom all about it because soon after the trip she started asking me when I would be competing next.

Around that same time, we filmed a documentary on my life and story—The Story of Furious Pete—with Omni Television. I had always been very open with my story, and, as I started breaking records and rose through the ranks of competitive eating, I made a lot of news stories and started to do a lot of TV shows. The film companies started calling soon after. There were a few early offers, but I said no to each one because

I didn't really like the angles they wanted to take with the film. But one director, George, got it right, and he had the funds to support doing the project well.

The filming was intense at times. There were a lot of in-depth interviews with my family and me. It got pretty emotional at times during the filming, but the toughest moment came as I was standing over an enormous pile of ribs.

We did a couple charity stunts during the filming, and we capped them off by organizing a rib-eating contest to raise money for MS research. This cause was very near and dear to me since my mother has Multiple Sclerosis. The turnout was awesome. A ton of people came, we raised a lot of money, and the energy was buzzing. I kept glancing over at my mom as she took in the scene around us. The level of support we felt was really tremendous.

Then it was time to eat.

I took my place on the stage next to a 15-pound pile of ribs. The challenge was to finish every last one in 15 minutes or less. It was definitely one of my more grotesque undertakings. My emotions were running high though as I saw my mother standing next to my dad in the crowd. It felt so good to be doing something so positive—to show that competitive eating *does* have a soul. We're not a bunch of crazy animals.

After I devoured the ribs in 13 minutes, I hopped off the stage to find my mother in the crowd. We were all in tears, hugging tightly.

She kissed me on the cheek and said, "That was great." It was all I could do to keep it together as the cameras rolled.

The documentary was well received. It made it into eight different film festivals around the world, including the Hot Docs film festival where it came in 6th place out of 200 films, and it still airs on Canadian television on a weekly basis. I enjoyed the experience far more than I expected, but the real gift was that moment with my mom.

CHAPTER 25

EATING IS A SPORT

I love competitive eating, but I have a huge passion for fitness. Fitness saved my life.

I started weight training and working out when I was in high school. Our school had a little weight room, and, as an extra part of gym class, we were able to have access to it once we learned how to lift properly. I got into it right away.

I was always a big skier, so initially I started training legs more than anything else, which was unusual for most of the students using the gym who were just there to build out their biceps and other beach muscles. I didn't give much thought to that kind of training—which is probably why those guys were the ones with girlfriends and I was the one with the quads. (I don't think I put two and two together at the time.) I wanted to be a hit with the ladies, of course, but my focus was elsewhere at the time.

While skiing and leg strength was my initial lens into fitness, I really got into it as a way to recover physically and mentally from one of the hardest experiences of my life. Fitness was my way of recovering from my eating disorder. It became a healthy outlet and a way to rebuild my body.

At first, I didn't necessarily know what to do, and I was really weak. I started reading fitness magazines, online articles, and watching demonstration videos to help me learn about different exercises. And then, one day at a time, I started going to the gym. It was all about experimentation and trying different things at the start, especially things that would help me put on healthy weight. And little by little, as I progressed, working out helped strengthen me both physically and mentally. Still, I would struggle, particularly when I felt stressed out, but I never quit.

I would tell myself, "Okay, it's time to go to the gym. You're going to feel better," and afterwards I would. Lifting a heavy weight over my head worked wonders for my stress levels, and, over time, it became a passion.

It wasn't about trying to form my physique or make myself look a certain way, it was more trying to lift heavy, to have fun in the gym, and focusing on trying to get stronger. I was working toward a positive goal to do something better, and that has always been my goal in life, no matter what I'm pursuing, to try to get better at that one thing.

When you get into fitness, obviously diet comes into play. A lot of people, particularly in the bodybuilding community, will start dieting and then become really anal about it. I had just come from years of obsessively monitoring my eating, and it was not a place I wanted to go back to.

As a side note: when people learn that I eat competitively, they naturally assume that it's something I do all the time or that my diet is terrible all the time. I can always tell when they are because I see them give a quick glance at my body, looking for the lingering effects of eating 200 chicken wings in a sitting. It's an easy assumption to make, I suppose, especially if they've seen my YouTube channel. I guess it's not a huge stretch to think that I do eating contest day in and day out, 24/7. I want to emphasize that I don't eat crazy every single day, and if I did, I would look the part. That said, I'm probably the only fitness dude online that is very proud to post pictures of myself having a beer. Everyone else is like, "No, no, I can't do that. That's bad. That's bad."

Here's the thing: it's all about balance, in life in general. It doesn't have to be fitness. It doesn't matter what you are doing, but if you start becoming too occupied, too anal about fitness, about working, about your physique, or about getting stronger, about anything like that, you are simply going to break down. You're not going to be as successful as you could be. If you let yourself go here and there, give yourself some freedom, let yourself in the fitness world, cheat on your diet, go out with friends, have a drink, or if you want to eat that, eat that, but that's just going to help you to stay on the right path and enjoy life. Because we are brought into this world where there are so many opportunities, so many possibilities, so many experiences and then if you become too anal about a certain activity, in this case fitness, then you're not going to experience all these wonderful things that you possibly could experience.

When I was doing eating contests on a weekly basis, I'd have to obviously prepare my body and prepare my mind for the competition, and I do that by heading straight for the gym. Working out does increase your appetite, after all. It definitely does for me. I train really hard to keep my body healthy in the face of eating 200 chicken wings.

It became even more crucial when I was out traveling. It's a little more difficult to maintain a balanced lifestyle when you're on the road, *especially* in the days after an eating contest when I'm dealing with the—ahem—fallout from it. It only took a couple instances of testing the fortitude of foreign toilets before I decided that I needed to have a plan in place.

Figuring out what that plan needed to be was easier said than done, however. First, I tried ice cream, thinking that it was liquid but dense and that must make it the perfect prep for my stomach. I was on a trip to an eating contest about a 12-hour drive from my city, and I stopped at McDonald's every 3 hours to get some ice cream cones. By the time I got there, I was so cracked out on sugar that I could barely fall asleep.

Then there was water training, which I thought was the trick used by all the greats to train for their big contests. In order to be on top, to be the best, I won't name names, but just in order to be the best, this is what they do. They drink a ton of water, really, really fast. 3 gallons of water in 3 minutes. And then vomit. And they will do that several times a day so that they keep their stomachs really elastic and make sure they can take in the appropriate volume that you need to take in.

I tried this trick a couple times. I felt so nauseous after just a few rounds that I chose to stop. It seemed dangerous and I felt terrible. If you don't know what you're doing – if you just drink a lot of water to see what drinking 3 gallons of water is like – you can throw up you can be in a lot of trouble. I didn't feel right doing it, so I never did it again.

Through a little trial and error, I worked out a pre- and post-challenge "training" regimen to prepare my body for what I was about to do to it. Before a challenge, I'll switch into a liquid diet for about a day and a half. And by liquid diet, I don't just mean water. It'll be like any kind of food that will be basically depleted out of my body come eating contest. So, that means I opt for some milk, some whey protein, yogurt, and stuff that will give my body the energy it will need to function after the challenge and work out whatever the competition food is.

I also want to make sure that I'm not eating anything prior to the challenge that will still be sitting in my body come contest time. If I were to eat a couple of steaks beforehand, they would likely still be hanging out in my body, taking up space that I need to win a challenge. Obviously, that's not going to help me at all. Hence the pre-challenge liquid diet.

I'm also going to be increasing my fluid intake after I do the contest. Then, after a day or so, it's really just back to normal.

I never try to starve myself before or after a challenge; that would be insane and probably damaging. I usually increase my fluid intake a little bit more to flush out extra sodium and anything else that's in my body if I just want to feel better.

Sometimes, the next day you'll be tired and go into the gym, and sometimes that is not possible. Some people online think that I'll have like a crazy meal or crazy contest, and I'll have super, super human powers to go to the gym. The truth is you get pretty sluggish if you have excess calories. So, I'll go back to the gym on a weekly basis when I'm not competing, which is very common right now.

The only time that I really do videos is for TV shows that I'm doing for Guinness World Records or for just eating challenges that I'll do online. But more commonly, believe it or not, I'll do a bunch of challenges day after day so that I have content the entire month. That way, I can focus on eating and focus on training and maintaining a healthy lifestyle for the rest of the time.

It took time for me to figure out what I needed to do for my body, to understand what I was depleting and what I needed to put back in after a challenge. It certainly was not an easy Google: "I just ate a 15-pound burger, like now I feel crappy, what do I do?" It was purely through trial and error. I didn't do any research or talk to anyone online. I simply tried out these things on myself. If they worked, great; if they didn't, lose them. I made a bunch of mistakes over the years, but, eventually, I found a solution that worked for me. I feel like that mentality really pushed me and got me going and made myself feel better.

And that includes trips to the gym, which are *ugly* in the days following back-to-back challenges. You're bloated, you're sluggish, and you have excess sodium; you have excess everything, really, and it takes a few days to recover. It's just a cruel fact that I can prepare myself for and make sure that I am mentally ready for a tough day of physical exercise. It takes preparation, and that didn't really hit home for me until I started treating my eating with the key principles of fitness. In other words, until I started treating competitive eating as an actual sport.

I started to look at water intake, the importance of breath, even form in my competitive eating the same way I would if I were assessing athletic performance and training.

I realized that breathing properly is key, and that takes being able to breathe properly in order to keep doing competitive eating. Eating contests are exhausting in a way that I never would have expected until I started doing them. There's no way for anyone to realize how exhausting ten minutes of fast eating is until they've done it. It may be over so quickly, but it's so exhausting that by the end of that ten minutes, you are really tired. And being able to breathe properly and being able to know your body and knowing the tempo you should be breathing is very, very important, and I think it can greatly affect your performance if you can breathe right.

Then there's the mental aspect of getting through an actual contest, and it starts with pushing yourself. From an athletic perspective, I look at this as if, say, you're in the gym, and you try to push heavy weights. You don't know whether you'll be able to get the weight over your head, but you're going to try. Sometimes you might have to take 5 minutes to focus, breathe, and clear your mind. Sometimes you might not get it done, and sometimes you might. If you're confident and you're ready for it, you know you can lift whatever weight you can lift up, and that's discipline to keep pushing even though you can't, telling yourself, "I can do another," in the middle of a circuit.

That is mind over matter, and it works the same way in competitive eating as it does in the gym. You get full, but you have to tell yourself, "Slowly, you can do this, and we can get through this one burger at a time. Breathe slowly, eat, drink, eat, drink." Just make sure you have the rhythm. Sometimes you have to take 5 minutes just to breathe as well. They definitely go hand in hand. Utilizing and improving these skills—whether through fitness or something like competitive eating—will strengthen your mind, shaping it into something very powerful and far more capable of withstanding the blows life can throw at you.

Fitness saved my life. It is the thing that gives me peace of mind. It is a place where I could go to and no one bothers me, and I am able to work out. That is pretty much what is it now, a place where I've got to go. I don't know how I found a sense of joy in lifting. It just makes me happy, and you can rarely find an activity in this world that will make you feel happy. You know some people love to play computer games and that makes them happy. Some people I know like to do yoga; some people I know get some massages. There's a whole list of hobbies out there to get excited about, and I would encourage anyone to go out and find what excites them.

And if that hobby, that activity, is there when hard times come your way, and you feel nothing else is going right, then take solace in your hobby. Know you're still doing something right, and you will develop a sense of respect for it. I know that from experience.

A lot of people think I went from one extreme to another, swinging from having an eating disorder to eating huge quantities of food competitively. I can't tell you how many comments I get that say something along the lines of "Overcompensate much?" or "This guy has clearly traded one extreme for another." And that's all some people think is going on. I don't see it that way at all, and when asked, I address it by pointing out the fact that I discovered this talent of mine after recovering for 3.5 years and being completely healthy mentally and physically for one. I've now been healthy for over a decade, thanks in large part to the personal growth that came from my experience with competitive eating.

If you discovered a talent that you're better at than 99.9999 percent of the world, you'd be stupid not to pursue it. The fact is, competitive eating is my job. I don't do it every day. I do contests when I have to do contests. Outside of that, I have a normal life, eat well, and go to the gym. I don't come home and eat a stack of ten pizzas.

Judging my move into competitive eating the way some people have (especially in my earlier days) is, I suppose, understandable if you don't get to know my story. In reality, however, those presumptions are wrong. If I moved from one extreme to another, I moved from being in extremely poor health to being in extremely good health. I moved from abusing my body to dedicating myself to taking care of it. I moved from an extremely negative outlook and isolation to a positive perspective and close relationships with those I love and care about.

Competitive eating may seem silly as far as professions go, but it has taught me a lot and given a lot to me as well. So has fitness. It built the business I have now, and it saved my life when I was younger. It saved my life. It makes me happy. And as far as professions (and passions) go, I couldn't ask for better.

In 2013, I started dedicating myself to doing more to promote fitness and overall good health as the days go on—and as the years go on. I knew what I wanted to do with the rest of my life: I wanted to impact people positively with my stories and any helpful advice I could offer, and I intended to do that through fitness. Little did I know, my first big opportunity to do so would actually come from illness—another cancer diagnosis. And this time, it was real.

CHAPTER 26

CANCER II

I was diagnosed the third week in September 2014, the tenth anniversary of my journey to recovery from anorexia.

A few weeks before that, I had noticed growth in one of my testis. It was problematic (in that it was there in the first place). "That can't be right," I thought to myself, and I immediately sat down at my computer to try to figure out what was going on. I started looking online to see if it could be what I thought it could be.

I didn't even know what kind of symptoms I was looking for. I didn't know any terms. Even with my rudimentary medical vocabulary, the search results all seemed to point to the same thing: testicular cancer.

Admittedly, despite having had a cancer scare when I was young, I had never taken the time to educate myself on what to look for, the benefits of early detection, or even to figure out how common cancer, especially testicular cancer, is. What I learned shocked me: one in 300 men will have testicular cancer. The stats were astonishing, yet until that day, I had never considered that I could get it.

(Almost immediately I felt compelled to share this information with anyone who would listen. I later filmed a video for YouTube, sharing what I had learned and encouraging others to be vigilant about early detection. I know a lot of people who watched my video and afterwards commented that, like me, they had never processed it in their head that they can get cancer. You can. Get checked.)

When I saw that one symptom of testicular cancer could be little bumps that you could feel, my heart started to beat faster. I had bumps, but not like what the text was describing. "No, that can't be what this is," I thought. "One of the bumps is four times greater than the other." I didn't see anything else listed that matched what I had, and, by virtue of the fact that I was scared of the possibilities running through my head, I decided to end my search. "What I have isn't a cancer symptom," I thought, and tried to think about something else while I waited for the bumps to go away.

But they didn't.

"Yeah, so this doesn't look right. What could it be?" I asked several of my friends over the course of the following week. The answer was the same across the board: a shake of the head and, "Go to the doctor, dude. Be sure." I knew I couldn't bury my head in the sand any longer. I called, made an appointment, and went in the very next day.

Flashbacks of the inconclusive test results I received as a kid came flooding back to me when the doctor looked at me and said, "I don't know what it can be. It's either swollen, filled with fluid, or something else. I have no idea. Or it could be something else a lot more serious. It could be something worse. We'll have to run some tests."

I was terrified. I had to push back getting an ultrasound because I had already committed myself to going to a fitness expo several cities away. I spent the entire weekend in a state of jittery paranoia, my thoughts consumed (again) with some very scary questions: Do I have cancer? If so, how bad is it? What will treatment be like? Will I be able to keep working?

Somehow I made it through the weekend. Come Monday, I was sent to an ultrasound to see what was going on. Fortunately, I didn't have to wait for weeks after the ultrasound to get my answer. I didn't even have to wait a day. I got a call 45 minutes later, which is unusually fast.

"Peter, you're going to need to come back in and see us immediately."

When I got the office, the receptionist showed me right into the doctor's personal office. There, he sat me down, and he told me, "It's not good news." He began to lay out next steps. I didn't really know how to process the news at that point.

I could only listen to what he was saying and try to keep it all straight.

He said, "We need you to go and see a specialist right away. I am going to book you an appointment as fast as I can. I'll make as many calls as I can and make sure you get seen as soon as possible."

By the time I left his office, I had an appointment already made with a specialist for the next day. Now my mind started racing again, moving in a million different directions but going nowhere. Finally, one thought stuck out in the noise: I have to call my parents.

Telling my mom and dad my bad news was extraordinarily hard, especially when I didn't have any concrete information to give them yet. I knew it was cancer, but I didn't know much else. My end of the conversation consisted mostly of "I don't know" and "We'll see," while my parents were focused on keeping it together so that they could support me and give me what I needed.

"Have you talked to Melissa yet?" my mom asked.

"Not yet. I'm not sure if now is the time."

My girlfriend, Melissa, had been out of town for several weeks already. She was in Texas for firefighter training, a task that required her full attention and investment if she was going to do well there. I knew that if I told her, all of her training would go to shit. I explained this to my mom, and, by the time

I stopped talking, I had resolved myself to keep quiet about what was going on until Melissa came home.

It was awful to keep this secret from her, especially when we spoke on the phone later that night. I tried to keep the conversation focused on her and what she was doing, but, inevitably, she swung it back towards me. "So, how are things with you?"

"Good. The fitness expo went super smooth..."

I went in for a second ultrasound, this time with the specialist, and as I had feared, the news was not good. The doctor nodded his head abruptly after he made his determination and told me, "Okay, we need to get you into surgery as fast as possible." I had a surgery booked less than a week later.

Melissa came home the next day. My heart was pounding when I picked her up from the airport that evening. Now that she was right in front of me, I had no idea how to even start the conversation. What was I supposed to say? *Hey, I'm so glad you're back. By the way, don't make any plans for Monday because I'm having cancer surgery.* So instead, I just kept letting her talk, asking more about her training and telling her how proud I was of her for all the work she had done.

When we got home, she went into the room and started unpacking, while I sat on the couch and psyched myself up to tell her. I heard her phone ring and then could hear her end of the conversation with her friend. "Yeah, that sounds awesome. Count us in. Great! See you in an hour!"

She walked back out into the living room where I was sitting. "That was Ashley. She and Nick are going out with some friends downtown and invited us to come. First round's on them in celebration of my illustrious return." Then she took a look at my face and added, "What? What's wrong?"

There was no backing down now. I replied, "Come sit next to me for a second." Then I told her everything. She cried like crazy and immediately starting trying to think of what she needed to do to help me. She quickly realized that she had no clue what to do and then started crying more. I had been worried that when I did tell her the truth, she would be angry that I had withheld something so big. And she was, a little bit, but she was also thankful.

Her response when I explained why I kept the cancer a secret from her was, "I wish you had told me, but then again, I'm glad you didn't." Then she went back to crying. I could barely keep it together. Melissa was terrified, and I was gutted. It was like my whole world was getting crushed as I held her.

"Oh my god," she said sitting up quickly. "I have to call Ash back and tell her that we aren't coming out to meet them."

"We can still go," I said.

"No. No way. I don't want to go anywhere. I just want to be with you."

As bad as the moment was, it was also hugely impactful for us in a very positive way. I could see how strong our relationship really was and how much we meant to each other. Melissa was right next to me for every step of the way from that day forward.

I went in for surgery on September 30th. My left testicle was removed, and, by all accounts, the surgery went very well. I went into an appointment a couple months later and was told my CT scans were clear. There was some hesitation about my right testicle, but there was no indication that it was going to present me with any problems.

So, I started to move forward with my life and thought everything was going to be okay. After months of worry and stress, I felt like I could take the experience for what it was, work to build awareness among my fans and community, and get back in the groove of my life. And it was awesome—for two weeks.

I went for another appointment and was told they weren't certain about a few things they were seeing in the CT scan. Some of my lymph nodes were a little bit enlarged. At least, they appeared to be. The docs weren't exactly certain about what it could be, so they couldn't give me a straight answer. Once again, I didn't know whether I was in the clear or simply waiting to find out what stage I was in.

I felt like I had been thrown right back to square one. The possibility that my cancer wasn't gone had been the last thing that was on my mind at that point—after my surgery and clean CT scans I thought I was done. So, it was a punch in the face to hear that I might not be clear yet. "A punch in the face" isn't even the right phrase. A punch is a quick shot of pain; it zaps around your body and then goes away. This was deeper. Heavier. Then the pain sharpened as I was told that I wasn't cleared, and we had to do more tests.

At this point, it brought me really down because I was being very optimistic and then, all of a sudden, it just...I just thought that maybe I'm going to have to go through a big process now and any goals that I had, any influence I had on a lot of people would fade out. "Maybe I won't be able to be as strong through another round of treatment," I worried. I had to go through a CT scan. Then another ultrasound to see if everything was okay with my right testicle. Then I had to wait.

During this time I took to YouTube to get the word out and raise a little awareness and offer a little education to my followers and everyone else I could reach. After all, I didn't think about checking down there until I found bumps. It didn't even occur to me, and I wish it had because it's so, so important.

Unfortunately, as important as it is, cancer screening for men just isn't really talked about—especially for younger guys. As a male, you're supposed to be looking around to these things, but word just isn't spreading the way it needs to. When it comes to raising awareness, only breast cancer gets the kind of attention it needs. And while they are important, of course, they are so female-centric that it doesn't feel like they're talking to men at all. I had seen those campaigns thousands of times, yet I never thought that their advice could pertain to me. Making this video and doing what I could to raise awareness was an opportunity to start the conversation.

If I was able to get one guy to check himself out by sharing on YouTube what was going on with me, then I wanted to do it. Still, I was nervous to post it. It had been years since I had shared something so personal online.

I told myself, "So, I have kind of grown up with YouTube. I've been really open about my life and have shared a lot of tough stuff. My fans are following me because I am open about what my life is actually like. This time shouldn't be any different." The mini-pep-talk worked. I reminded myself that I wanted to help others. I chose to be open about it from the beginning, rather than wait for it to come out on its own or through someone else. I felt like I could help my viewers more by speaking to them directly, letting them know that I was scared and being honest about the fact that I didn't know what was next.

I showed the video to Melissa that night. I was nervous even to show her.

When the clip ended, she turned to me and wrapped her arms around me. "You've come a long way, you know?"

"What do you mean?" I asked her.

"I mean when you were misdiagnosed with cancer when you're younger, it threw you in an entirely different direction. You felt like you couldn't control anything, so you found an area that you felt like you could control and clung to it even though it was hurting you. Even though it was so detrimental to your health, you grasped on to that and turned inward."

"Yeah, I guess, but I was kid."

She continued, paying little regard to my attempt to offset what she was saying. "Whereas with this diagnosis, which was a true diagnosis, it wasn't a mistake, and you moved in the opposite direction. You turned your focus outward, toward helping other people. Instead of keeping your pain a secret, you opened it up for others to connect to—even though you were scared."

"I guess I'm stronger now than I was then. I hope I still will be when this is all over with."

It was three weeks, almost a month, of just hesitation. Honestly, I doubted myself. I didn't think I'd be getting good news. When I went back in to meet with my doctors, I went in there with a mindset that I still had cancer; my focus more was trained on what my treatment would look like. I was foreseeing the future and thinking, "Okay, I'm going to have to go through X amount of months of treatment, and this is what it's going to look like. Maybe my hair will fall out." I could picture myself without hair. "I'm not going to be able to do this kind of TV show anymore. I'm not going to be able to be working out like I wanted to. I won't be able to do this." I had a lot of thoughts going through my head as to what my new reality was going to be like. But lucky for me, the appointment brought good news: my latest scans were clear.

I was thrilled, of course, but the mental body slam of doubting myself and my future stuck with me for a while. As optimistic as I'd like to be, as positive as I would like to be, it can be really hard, and there's nothing wrong with that. It's perfectly understandable and probably something I should have allowed myself to feel more. I just didn't think about that. I didn't pay any attention to how I was actually feeling before and after my surgery. I launched straight into trying to raise awareness and trying to help others, rather than focus some efforts on myself and make sure that I was okay mentally. I've learned that it's my go-to move when my life takes a sharp turn into a crisis.

Most of the time, whenever I do have a dramatic or troubling experience in my life, I try to create positives auras for people around me rather than myself, while pushing my own feelings and thoughts out of the way. I don't deal with them; I bury them. That's why the hesitation about whether I might still have cancer hit me like a sack of doorknobs, and that's why that feeling lingered even after I found out that I was okay.

When we got the news that I was clear, my mother and my girlfriend (now my fiancée) were jumping for joy around me. I felt separate from the whole scene, like I was looking at it from afar.

I don't think it really hit me until a few days later when I woke up early one morning. I sat up in my bed for 30 minutes just thinking about the fact that I was clear. I started thinking about other people that have gone through treatment, about the impact it had on their bodies and minds. Then I thought, "I don't need to go through the difficult treatment they did." I could continue on with my goals. I could continue on with life and really try to make a change for a lot of other people.

I could help other people's lives and make sure that if they approach or encounter negative issues and events in their life that they approach them in the appropriate way.

I got out of bed ready to do an entire transformation, and that's where I am now. I'm trying to get in the best shape of my life by dieting and working out as hard as I can. I want what I do to create a message that is as positive as possible.

I want people to know that life is short. We've heard these messages all the time. It's very redundant. Very cliché. I'm not talking about it in a "what would you do if you only had a year left" kind of way. I'm not telling you to go skydiving or anything crazy—not at all. To me, the "life is short" message is a reminder to be aware whether we're spending our time feeling good or bad.

One of the biggest things I've learned from all this is that we don't have a ton of time on this planet, and the time we do have is finite. So, it makes *zero* sense to move through that time feeling terrible and letting the little inconveniences and obstacles that pop into your life bother you. You miss the bus, or you shattered your phone, or you lose $200 in the casino, or you just fail at something. This stuff happens all the time! The way I see it, there are two ways of approaching the things that make you feel like crap. You can either take the left road or you can take the right road. The left road means taking it in a very negative way and letting it ruin your day, your week, and possibly your month or let it impact even your relationships through your sour mood. Or you can take the right road, which would be not letting it bother you. Choose to focus on the important things: your family, your health, your friends, and your future.

No matter which road you choose, it will lead to bigger things. Focusing on the positive important things in your life will lead to bigger and more positive things. Do the opposite, like I feel a lot of people in this world do, and the negative things in your life can spiral into bigger, much more negative things. I've lived that negative spiral plenty of times, and I don't think that should ever be the approach. I've made the choice to go in both directions over the course of my life, and I know from experience that if you take that route where you don't let these things bother you, you find more peace in your life. You can really appreciate more and be able to accomplish more.

And if you really don't like something you've got going in your life, change it. I've been talking about this even before my diagnosis. You've probably heard it before, if not from me then from someone else. If there's something that you're doing in your life that you don't enjoy or if it is dragging you down—a job, a relationship, whatever it may be—then you really need to make a change in your life. Figuring out what you want to change and how you can change it is really tough, but look at the things that make you feel good and positive as your clues. Make the ways you fill your time better so that you are enjoying the time that you have.

On the other hand, if you're already doing what makes you feel good, keep doing it. Once, when we were in a restaurant in Warsaw, I got into a conversation with our waiter about how much he loves his job. This guy *loved* waiting tables and wouldn't have traded up to do anything else. It was the exact opposite of the way I think a lot of us view other jobs, whether it's serving, teaching, or working in finance. It's easy to look at other jobs and say, "I wouldn't want do that for more than a year. Maximum," and in doing so, we discount the value that it might hold for others—or worse, we make them feel bad about wanting to be where they are. Or maybe we listen to that kind of negative feedback, internalize it, and start to doubt whether we should do something "safer," "smarter," or "better," instead of doing what we love.

Do what makes you happy, and if you're not happy with what you're doing, then change it. If you *are* happy, keep pursuing what you're doing—even if everyone else around you tells you you're crazy for doing so.

I get a lot of hate because of what I do online. I've learned over time that haters just come with the territory of having a public presence. It wasn't easy at first, but I've figured out that I can just put a barrier between them and me. You can have a lot of haters out there, but if you're truly passionate and confident about what you're doing, and you feel like this is the right thing for you, and you know that what you're doing is going to make a change in other people's lives or it's going to make changes in your life, then do it. If it makes your life happy, then keep doing it because that's what matters. If other people want to spin their wheels over what you're doing, let them—but don't let them stop you.

These messages were things I had believed for years, but as I sat in my room that morning just a few days after getting the all-clear signal, they became totally solidified for me. I guess scary or dramatic events have a way of doing that. Those kinds of experiences can add another layer to your understanding, to the way you approach different things, and to the way you approach life. I think that's what happened for me during my diagnosis, surgery, scare, and then in the emotional fallout that came after it all. I had to sit down and remind myself that I'm alive.

I still do that too. When I catch myself stressing out or getting bogged down by the obstacles and frustrations that swing my way, I sit down and remind myself that I can still do the things that I want to do. I have a to be grateful for it and know I am blessed for that. That's the lesson that I've been learning, and that's what I'm taking away from it. I'm just able to sit down and remind myself what it means to be able to live life to the fullest—what it means to stay hungry and be dedicated for life.

Staying hungry means that no matter how big your goals are, no matter how big the struggle is, no matter how many obstacles you have or what's in the way, if you have your mind in the right place, if you have the right game plan, you can always succeed.

Maybe being successful doesn't mean achieving your goal fully. It means you can always just succeed in achieving part of that success. Maybe it's going to take a very long time to achieve that success, but if you just tell yourself, "Yeah, no, I can't do it. It's too hard," or, "There's all this other stuff I have to do first," you're never going to achieve what you want. But if you are hungry for those goals, if you're hungry for success, or if you're hungry for recovery or whatever it is that your goals are, then you can really achieve anything.

Dedicated for life, in short, means that you are simply dedicated to every task that you take on. It can apply to your whole life, or it can apply to something that you're doing for the next hour. So, if you are going to the gym, you're dedicating yourself to making sure you're going to function, and you're going to do the very best that you can for the next hour with that activity. So, what I like to tell people is just to put yourself in that state of mind that you can, if you plan it right, and if you do it right, and if you're smart about it, you really can achieve everything.

I think "Stay hungry" and "Dedicated for life" go hand in hand in trying to push individuals to be the best they can and live the best they can. If you feel what you're doing is right and you want to do it, then live by those two mottos. Staying hungry and dedicated for life. They will take you places.

ABOUT THE AUTHOR

Pete Czerwinski is a professional competitive speed eater and a fitness athlete. His YouTube videos show off his skills in both eating and fitness.

He currently hosts a TV show for German TV, holds numerous Guinness World Records, is a sponsored athlete, a M,Eng in Manufacturing and posts regularly on YouTube.

PHOTOS

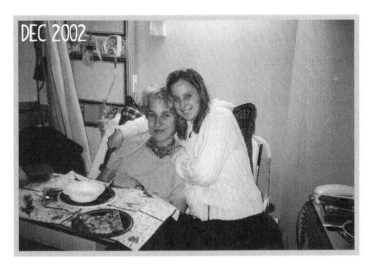

Hospitalized for Anorexia at 120lbs, near fatal heart rate, life support

Hospitalized for Anorexia at 120lbs, near fatal heart rate, life support

(*left*) 2 months out from Hospital, 140lbs, huge fear of food still
(*right*) 18 Months out of the hospital

My first eating contest – Collegiate Nationals in San Diego, California. I killed the competition then won 20+ contests in a row after.

My first **FAILED** eating challenge. They screwed me. Clinton Station Diner

Filming the first world tour episode with German TV. Huge Burger in Berlin, Germany, it was 30lbs and I ate half of it.

Filming with German TV again in the Austrian Alps

Outside of the famous Randy's Donuts in LA filming with German TV

Filming in Sochi, Russia right before the Olympics

Filming in Beijing (Great Wall of China Featured)

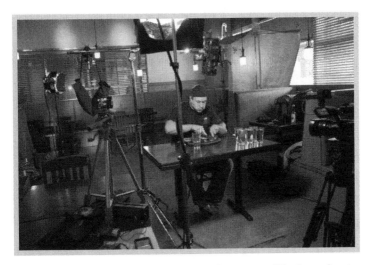

Filming a 72oz Steak eat in record time for my documentary "The Story of Furious Pete"

Eating Contest Picture. This was the Go Go Curry contest in NYC.

En Route to winning my 3rd or 4th Z-Burger Eating Championship in
Washington, DC

Another Eating Contest picture hot dog

Competing against Takeru Kobayashi (photo by Toronto Star)

Competing against Takeru Kobayashi (photo by Toronto Star)

My million subscriber video special with 5lbs of Nutella and answering questions

d4L. Dedicated For Life. My trademark motto that I live by every day of my life. Regardless of what I am doing, I dedicate myself 100% towards that activity/goal.

Picture from photoshoot in April after doing a transformation months after having Cancer. Tried to show the world what I'm made of.

Picture from photoshoot in April after doing a transformation months after having Cancer. Tried to show the world what I'm made of.

Team Furious Logo

Printed in Great Britain
by Amazon